WITNESS LEE

THE ULTIMATE
SIGNIFICANCE
OF THE
GOLDEN
LAMPSTAND

Living Stream Ministry

Anaheim, CA • www.lsm.org

First Edition, March 1998.

ISBN 978-0-7363-0304-0

Published by

Living Stream Ministry
1853 W. Ball Road, Anaheim, CA 92804 U.S.A.
P. O. Box 2121, Anaheim, CA 92814 U.S.A.

Printed in the United States of America

15 16 17 18 19 20 / 10 9 8 7 6 5 4

CONTENTS

PREFACE

This book is a translation of messages given in Chinese by Brother Witness Lee in an international conference held by the church in Taipei, Taiwan, on October 19 through 22, 1977.

CHAPTER ONE

THE SIGNIFICANCE
OF THE GOLDEN LAMPSTAND

Scripture Reading: Exo. 25:31-32, 36-37; Zech. 4:2, 10b; Rev. 1:12-13, 20; 4:5b; 5:6; 1:4

In this book we will specifically consider the golden lampstand in the Bible. Apparently, the Gospel, the Epistles, and the Revelation written by John are unrelated to the book of Exodus in the Old Testament; or we may say that it is difficult to find the relationship between them. It is as if the former were "wearing Western attire" and the latter "Chinese gowns" so that no one can see the relationship between them. However, I want to make it clear that in substance John's writings are the development of Exodus.

THE RELATIONSHIP BETWEEN JOHN'S WRITINGS
AND THE BOOK OF EXODUS

The Lamb and the Tabernacle

There are several important items in the book of Exodus. The first item is the passover lamb. The book of Exodus is called *Exodus* because the passover lamb enabled the children of Israel to go out of Egypt. The second item is the tabernacle. After the children of Israel kept the passover, left Egypt, and reached the wilderness, God wanted them to build a tabernacle for Him. Hence, when we come to the end of Exodus in chapter 40, we see a tabernacle erected and filled with the glory of God. Thus, we see that the first main item in Exodus is the lamb, and the last main item is the tabernacle. Now I would like to ask, in John's Gospel, Epistles, and Revelation, what are the first and last main items? In John's writings there are two "beholds." In John 1 there is one "behold": "Behold, the Lamb of God, who takes away the sin of the world!" (v. 29), and in Revelation 21 there is another "behold": "Behold, the tabernacle of God is with men" (v. 3). In Exodus there are the lamb and the tabernacle, and the lamb is for the tabernacle. Likewise, in John's writings there are the Lamb and the tabernacle, and the Lamb is also for the tabernacle.

The Holy Anointing Oil

Between the lamb and the tabernacle there are several other items, one of which is the holy anointing oil. This holy anointing oil is found in Exodus and also in John's Epistles. The anointing that John spoke of was not invented by him; rather, he took it from Exodus. However, if we read only John's Epistles, we may know about the holy anointing oil itself but not its ingredients. If we want to know its ingredients, we have to go back to Exodus. There we find that one of its ingredients is a hin of olive oil; this is the base. Added to this hin of olive oil are four kinds of spices: five hundred shekels of myrrh, two hundred fifty shekels of fragrant cinnamon and two hundred fifty shekels of fragrant calamus, and five hundred shekels of cassia. The two units of two hundred fifty shekels form one combined unit of five hundred shekels. These are the constituents of the holy anointing oil. Four kinds of spices are added to, compounded into, the olive oil as the base. Thus, the oil is no longer merely oil but has become an ointment. Furthermore, the measurements of the ingredients signify the Triune God, of whom the second was split. The number five signifies God the Creator with man the creature. The second unit being split implies Christ's death. Furthermore, calamus, which grows in a marsh or muddy place, signifies resurrection, and the fragrance of cassia has the power to repel poisonous insects. When we add all these items together, we can see the elements and the functions of the holy anointing oil.

The Need to Study
the Old Testament "Classics"

From the foregoing points, we can see that it is not enough for us to have only the New Testament; we also need the Old

Testament. In the New Testament we can see the holy anointing oil, the anointing, but we cannot find its ingredients and its functions. To find its ingredients and functions we have to go to the "classics" to find the original picture. Where are the "classics"? One of the classics is Exodus. The entire book of Exodus is a classical book. What does "Behold, the Lamb of God!" mean? We find the answer in the classics. After some searching, we find in Exodus 12 that every house had to prepare a lamb. In addition, Revelation 21:3 says, "Behold, the tabernacle of God is with men." What does this mean? Again, we need to go back to the classics. In Exodus we can see how the tabernacle was built, what kind of materials were used, and what kind of a situation was there. To find these matters, we must go back to the classics. Therefore, we all need to study the classical books.

THE GOLDEN LAMPSTAND BEING CHRIST AND ALSO BEING THE CHURCHES

Having seen the holy anointing oil in the classics, we now want to look at Revelation 1. There the apostle John said, "When I turned, I saw seven golden lampstands" (v. 12). To see what the lampstands are, we again need to turn to the classics. I do not know if you have ever looked into the classics about the lampstands. Again, I say to the young people, you must learn to study the classics. For example, if you want to have a good foundation in the Chinese language, you must study the Chinese classics; otherwise, you will only follow others by repeating what they say without understanding what you are saying. This is true also in spiritual things. Today, not to mention Christians in general, even theologians only follow what others have said.

The seven golden lampstands are the seven churches. Why is this? Most would say that it is because the lampstands give forth light, and the churches also give forth light and shine in today's dark age. This is to "parrot" what others say. The golden lampstands are not so simple; to know them we need to search the classics. The lamb, the tabernacle, and the holy anointing oil can be found in the classics; so also the golden lampstand is found in the classics. In Exodus we find not only the lamb and the tabernacle but also the holy anointing oil and the golden lampstand. Likewise, in John's writings we find not only the Lamb and the tabernacle but also the holy anointing oil and the golden lampstand. John's writings are the development of Exodus. Exodus is the seedbed, the nursery, with the seeds sown and the sprouts growing; John's writings are a big farmland, no longer a nursery. I encourage you to go back to study the classics and "dig in the nursery."

For seven and a half years I was with a Brethren assembly that was well versed in the Bible. I attended more than a thousand meetings there, and there was not one meeting in which we did not study the Bible or hear a message. They did not gossip, and they did not have much prayer and singing. Whenever they came together, they only read the Bible, studied the Bible, and expounded the Bible. I was with those teachers and was taught by them well over one thousand times. I cannot count how many times I heard about the tabernacle and the lamb. I also heard about the seventy weeks at the end of Daniel 9, the four beasts in Daniel 7, the two beasts in Revelation, and the great image in Daniel 2. Because I heard them speak for a full seven and a half years, from 1925 to the summer of 1932, I became so familiar and deeply impressed with these matters that even to this day I can recite the chapters and the verses. However, my point is this: After listening to so much, I only learned from the Brethren teachers that the golden lampstand signifies Christ as the light, because the Lord Jesus said, "I am the light of the world; he who follows Me shall by no means walk in darkness, but shall have the light of life" (John 8:12). I accepted their interpretation. Then after 1932 when the church was raised up in my hometown, Chefoo, I preached five times a week. I told others that the Lord Jesus is the golden lampstand, the light of the world, and that without Him we are in darkness but with Him we walk in the light. My preaching was bold and clear, and it was also very inspiring. Nevertheless, no one ever told me that the golden lampstand is related to the church. Actually, the golden lampstand is not only related to the church, but it is the church. Have you heard this before? Praise the Lord that we have heard this in the church throughout the past two years.

In Exodus the golden lampstand is Christ, but in the development in Revelation 1, the golden lampstands are no longer merely Christ but also the churches. In the nursery it is Christ, but in the farmland it is the churches. The golden lampstand has been expanded from one to seven. In Exodus there is one lampstand, but in Revelation there are seven lampstands. One lampstand is Christ, whereas the seven lampstands are the churches. Originally it was Christ alone, but Christ has become many churches. The Brethren teachers repeatedly taught that the tabernacle refers not only to Christ but also to the church; they were very clear concerning this matter. However, they never told people that the lampstand refers not only to Christ but also to the church. They did not have sufficient light concerning this matter. Thank the Lord, He has given us further light, which enables us to see that the golden lampstand is indeed Christ, but this Christ who is one has become many.

Upon hearing this, those who do not have the light of the subjective truth will say, "Witness Lee teaches heresy, saying that one Christ has become many Christs. Do we, then, have many Saviors?" This is not the proper way of reasoning. Christ, who is one, has become many, but Christ the Savior is unchanged. First Corinthians 12:12 says, "Even as the body is one and has many members, yet all the members of the body, being many, are one body, so also is the Christ." Can we change *so also is the Christ* to *so also is the Savior* or *so also is God*? Of course not, yet this is the method of argument generally used by the opposing ones in Christianity. I have told people in a definite way that Christ can increase from one to many, but some say that this is heresy because this makes one Savior many Saviors. Nevertheless, "All the members of the body, being many, are one body, so also is the Christ." This clearly tells us that today Christ is the Body, and since the Body is the church, Christ is also the church. In Exodus the golden lampstand, which is Christ, is uniquely one; in Revelation the golden lampstands being seven are many. In Exodus the lampstand is Christ, but in Revelation it has become the churches. If you do not agree with me, you should go back and have a quiet time to pray to the Lord; then He will give you the light to see that in the Old Testament the golden lampstand is Christ and that in the New Testament, especially at the end, the golden lampstands are the churches. In the Old Testament type, there was only Christ but not the church, but in the New Testament, Christ as the one grain of wheat has become many grains and as the one lampstand has become many lampstands. Instead of trying to argue with me, go back and pray quietly; the light will shine upon you so that you will see that today every proper local church is a golden lampstand. Just as Christ is the golden lampstand, so every local church is also a golden lampstand, exactly the same, without any difference.

More than forty years ago I had a wrong concept. I thought that the lampstand in the Old Testament consisted of one stand with seven lamps, but that the seven lampstands in Revelation consist of seven stands with a total of seven lamps. Now I would like to say that this is wrong. Each stand of the golden lampstands in Revelation has seven lamps. How can we prove this? The proof is in the sevenfold intensified Spirit. Over forty years ago I saw only the Holy Spirit but not the sevenfold intensified Spirit. Today, however, I clearly see that the lampstands in the New Testament are exactly the same as the lampstand in the Old Testament; they also consist of one stand with seven lamps each, and these seven lamps are the seven Spirits of God.

THE GOLDEN LAMPSTAND BEING THE TRIUNE GOD

The golden lampstand also signifies the Triune God. In the golden lampstand there is the number three. It has a shaft with six branches going out from its sides, three branches on the right side and three branches on the left side. Three signifies the Triune God. In addition, on the shaft and the branches of the lampstand there are three layers—the cups, the calyxes, and the blossom buds—which also signify the Triune God. Besides these, there are other features, which show us that the golden lampstand signifies the Triune God.

Its Substance Signifying God the Father

The golden lampstand is of pure gold, without any impurities. In biblical typology, gold denotes the divine nature. Just as the substance of a table is wood and the substance of a book is paper, so the substance of the golden lampstand is gold. Gold signifies the nature of God. With the exception of gold, every kind of metal is alterable. God's nature is like gold, which is unique, pure, rustproof, and unalterable. Therefore, the lampstand in its substance signifies God the Father; in the golden lampstand we see the substance, the nature, of God the Father.

Its Form Signifying God the Son

The golden lampstand is a stand with a form, and this form signifies Christ. Christ is the embodiment of God, and in Him dwells all the fullness of the Godhead bodily (Col. 2:9). Therefore, in the lampstand we see not only the substance, the nature, but also the form. A fragment, pile, piece, or lump of gold has no definite form. The one talent of gold in the golden lampstand, however, is not a pile of gold; it has a solid form, which signifies the incarnated Christ. In the incarnated Christ, the embodiment of God, all the fullness of the Godhead dwells bodily. Here, therefore, we have the nature of God the Father and the form of God the Son.

Its Expression Signifying God the Spirit

The golden lampstand has seven lamps. What are these seven lamps? We cannot find the full explanation in the Old Testament; there is a partial answer in the book of Zechariah, but it is not clear enough. Zechariah 4 says that the seven lamps on the lampstand are the seven eyes of God. Today in His administration and operation, God has seven eyes. Many Christians like to use pictures to express spiritual things, but I have never seen a picture that shows God as having seven eyes. According to our concept, how many eyes does God have? To be sure, we may say that He has two eyes, yet the Bible says that God has seven eyes. We cannot separate the seven eyes from God and "suspend them in the air." Therefore, because the seven lamps are the seven eyes of God, the seven lamps are God Himself. We must see that the golden lampstands are God.

The Bible is not so simple. When we come to Revelation, we

see that the seven lamps are not only the seven eyes but also the seven Spirits of God. The seven lamps are the seven eyes, the seven eyes are the seven Spirits of God, and the seven Spirits of God are the Holy Spirit. The Holy Spirit is the Spirit of God, and the Spirit of God is one. Why, then, does Revelation speak of seven Spirits? This may be likened to a light bulb with a brightness that can be adjusted and strengthened onefold, twofold, or threefold. If we do not need a very bright light, onefold is enough; if we need brighter light, we can increase the brightness to the second or third intensity. The Spirit of God is the lamp of God. In the severest darkness there is the need to intensify the light sevenfold. The time in which John wrote the book of Revelation was the darkest time. Today do we need the one Spirit or the seven Spirits? It is too dark today! We need the sevenfold intensified Spirit. How much light do we have in the local churches today? The light is sevenfold! Many can testify that since they came to the church, they have been under the constant shining of this light. This light is not a negligible light like the light of a firefly, a match, or a candle. Today the light in the local churches is a sevenfold intensified light.

Formerly, as a "churchgoer," a brother could strike his wife after coming home from a Sunday worship service and have no problem. But now after coming home from a meeting of the church and finding that his wife has done something wrong, as he is about to rebuke her, the light strongly shines on him. The light is so strong that his anger is dissipated. Sometimes a husband may speak a harsh word, but as the wife is about to talk back, the light shines strongly on her. It is for this reason that many of us can testify that since we came into the church, there is not much quarreling in our homes. This does not mean that we do not have opinions. Sometimes I have an opinion on the tip of my tongue concerning a certain person, but the light comes, and I say, "O Lord, I praise You! All things, even this misbehaving one, are mine. I thank and praise You, Lord, that all things work together for good to those who love God." In this way we do not quarrel.

In contrast, in many of the board meetings and meetings of the responsible ones in Christianity, there are frequent quarrels, sometimes openly and other times secretly. However, many of us can testify that it is not this way in the local churches. We thank the Lord for this! This is because in the churches the light is very strong. When we are about to quarrel, the light shines not only on our lips but also in the depths of our being. This sevenfold intensified light is stronger than any kind of x-ray. This is true not only in quarreling but also in many other matters. In the local churches the light is strong because there is the sevenfold intensified Spirit.

The substance of the golden lampstand is God the Father, its form is God the Son, and its expression is God the Spirit. The Father, the Son, and the Spirit are all here. When the Lord Jesus walked on the earth, He was the golden lampstand; wherever He went, the light shined. Matthew 4 tells us that when He went to Galilee in particular, a great light shined over those sitting in the region and shadow of death (v. 16). Moreover, while He was walking on the earth, He had a bodily form. Jesus Christ was that bodily form. The substance, the nature, within Him was God Himself, and the expression upon Him was the Spirit. The Triune God is the golden lampstand, and the golden lampstand is the Triune God.

THE FATHER, THE SON, AND THE SPIRIT
BEING INSEPARABLE

Today's Christianity still holds the traditional doctrine concerning the Trinity, saying that the Father is one entity, the Son is another, and the Spirit is still another. Many would say that the Father, the Son, and the Spirit are three different, separate entities. This shows that they are short of light. Revelation says that the Spirit of God as the seven Spirits is not only the seven eyes of God but also the seven eyes of the Lamb. The Lamb is Christ, and the seven eyes are the Holy Spirit. Can we say that a person's eyes and the person himself are two separate, independent entities? The seven Spirits of God as the Holy Spirit are the eyes of Christ as the Lamb. This tells us that the Holy Spirit and Christ cannot be divided, just as our eyes and our person cannot be separated. Likewise, the lamps and the lampstand cannot be divided. The seven lamps are the seven Spirits of God, so these seven Spirits cannot be separated from the lampstand. The Holy Spirit and Christ can never be divided. We must be deeply impressed that the lampstand in reality is the very Triune God, and all the fullness of the Godhead dwells bodily in Christ; this Christ has been expressed, and His expression is the sevenfold intensified Spirit.

Is the lampstand one or seven? It is both. According to its substance, the lampstand is one; according to its development, function, and administration, the lampstand is seven. Our God is the Triune God; He is the Father as the substance, the Son as the form, and the Spirit as the expression. The Father as the substance is in the Son as the form, and the Son as the form is expressed as the Spirit. A picture speaks far better than a thousand words. The Triune God is so exceedingly mysterious that we cannot describe Him with our human language. We cannot even describe the human face, so how can we describe the Triune God? Thanks be to God that there is a picture in the Bible! This picture is the lampstand—its substance is gold, its form is the stand, and its expression is the seven lamps. This is the picture of the Triune God.

While He was walking on the earth, the Lord Jesus was the Triune God. We can say this because He was the pure gold. Apparently, He was Jesus the Nazarene; actually, He was one talent of gold. You and I are so many pounds of clay; we may adorn ourselves to look very nice, but when anyone touches us, our clay is exposed. However, while the Lord Jesus was on the earth, no one could touch anything of clay in Him. On the contrary, the more people touched Him, the more shining and precious He was. Certain ones tested Jesus, as if to pour water on Him to see if He was clay, but the more people touched Him, the more shining He was, and the more they "poured water on Him," the brighter He became. When the Lord Jesus was on the earth, He went through the cities and villages. All kinds of people—Pharisees, Sadducees, Herodians, rabbis, elders, and scribes—came to touch Him and "pour water on Him," yet the more they touched Him, the more shining He was, and the more they "poured water," the brighter He became. He is pure gold. Not only so, as He stood in front of people, He was the light. He was the seven lamps; wherever He went, there was the sevenfold light. He was the golden lampstand, denoting the Triune God. The Father was there, the Son was there, and the Spirit was there; that is, the Father's substance was there, the Son's form was there, and the Spirit's expression and illumination were there. This is what Christ is.

THE CHURCH
BEING THE REPRODUCTION OF CHRIST

We praise the Lord that this Christ as the one grain of wheat was buried in the ground and died, and He resurrected to become many grains. After His death and resurrection the church was produced. He is uniquely one, but the churches are many; the church in each locality is an expression of Christ. Hence, one lampstand has become many lampstands. What is the church? The church is the reproduction of Christ. The one Christ has been reproduced through His death and resurrection. As Christ is, so is the church. This is not a doctrine but a subjective experience.

CHAPTER TWO

THE HOLY SPIRIT WITH CHRIST
FOR THE CHURCH

Scripture Reading: Exo. 25:31-32, 37; Zech. 3:9; 4:2-10; Rev. 1:4, 11-13, 20; 4:5; 5:6

THE DEVELOPMENT OF THE REVELATION
CONCERNING THE GOLDEN LAMPSTAND

The revelations in the Bible are progressive. Most of the revelations are sown as seeds in Genesis, they are developed little by little in the succeeding books, and they consummate in Revelation. We may say that in Genesis we have the seeds and in Revelation we have the harvest. The revelation concerning the golden lampstand, which is first mentioned in Exodus 25, is the same in principle. Here I must add a little word: The concept concerning the golden lampstand cannot be found in human history or in any human writings. It is a very particular matter. Not even an expert designer today could possibly create such a pattern. Hence, in the last several thousand years the golden lampstand has remained a unique matter that is not of human thought but of the divine conception. Therefore, this pattern is very special; it is one lampstand with seven lamps. Every item of this lampstand bears some spiritual meaning.

The golden lampstand is thoroughly covered in Exodus, but there is the need for further development. For example, in Exodus 25 the lampstand is spoken of as a beaten work of pure gold, but there is no mention of the oil. However, in Zechariah 4 something is added. It says that there are two olive trees by the sides of the lampstand, and at the end of chapter 4 the two olive trees are the two sons of oil. These two sons of oil are filled with oil. In Revelation 11 these two olive trees, the two sons of oil, are the two witnesses who are coming (vv. 3-4). After many believers are raptured to the heavens, the testimony of God on this earth will fall upon these two witnesses. We must see that the two witnesses in Revelation 11 are also two golden lampstands. The main point, however, is that in Exodus there is the golden lampstand but not the olive oil; it is in Zechariah 4 that the oil is mentioned. Concerning the lampstand with the two olive trees by its sides, the prophet Zechariah asks, "What are these, sir?" Then the angel answers, "Not by might nor by power, but by My Spirit, says Jehovah of hosts" (vv. 4, 6). This indicates that in Zechariah 4 the concept concerning the Spirit is brought in. In Exodus 25 there is only the concept concerning the gold—the golden lampstand—with no mention of the oil, but in Zechariah 4 the oil is mentioned. This oil is the Holy Spirit. First there is the golden lampstand, and then there is the olive oil (the Holy Spirit). Then in Revelation 1 we see that there is not just one golden lampstand but seven golden lampstands (v. 12). One has become many.

THE THREE STAGES OF THE SPEAKING
CONCERNING THE GOLDEN LAMPSTAND

The speaking concerning the golden lampstand in the Bible is in three stages: The first stage is the golden lampstand, the second stage is the golden lampstand with the olive oil (the Holy Spirit), and the third stage is the singular lampstand becoming the plural lampstands—one lampstand becoming many lampstands. This is very meaningful. In Exodus 25 the emphasis of the lampstand is on Christ; in Zechariah 4 the emphasis is on the Holy Spirit; and in Revelation 1 the emphasis is on the churches. All three passages mention the lampstand, but in the first passage Christ is emphasized, in the second passage the Holy Spirit is emphasized, and in the third passage the churches are brought forth.

How is the church brought forth? It is produced by having the Spirit in addition to Christ. Christ with the Spirit is the church as the golden lampstand. According to God's eternal desire, economy, or plan, the golden lampstand is not merely Christ or merely Christ with the Spirit; instead, the golden lampstand is Christ with the Spirit producing the church. The church is God's ultimate goal. God's plan is from Christ through the Spirit to the church. If there is Christ yet not the Spirit, God cannot carry out His plan; if there is Christ with the Spirit yet without the church, God has not yet reached the ultimate goal of His economy.

We need to see that when the lampstand is spoken of in the last book of the Bible, the emphasis is neither on Christ nor on the Spirit but on the church. Here I must speak a word that may make people unhappy; however, what is true is true and what is false is false, and what is good is good and what is bad is bad. I would be glad to say something good about others, and sometimes I have made up my mind and resolved that I would not mention Christianity in my preaching. However, while I am giving a message, I cannot help mentioning it because the anointing anoints me to do so. In the divine revelation, first there is Christ, then the Spirit, and eventually the church. However, is the reality of the church in today's Christianity? Absolutely not. Therefore, Christianity is really pitiful. There is even a group of so-called seekers of spirituality who say, "We only care for Christ; we don't care for the church." This has become their slogan. They want Christ but not the church; this means that they want Exodus but not Revelation. Does Revelation speak about Christ or the church? John did not say, "I turned and saw Christ." Rather, he said, "When I turned, I saw seven golden lampstands"; he also said, "In the midst of the lampstands One like the Son of Man" (1:12-13). This is a complete vision.

CARING FOR CHRIST AND THE CHURCH

Today we must see the church, and we must also see Christ walking in the midst of the churches. Many of us can testify that when we were in the denominations, we did not see much of Christ, nor did we enjoy much of Christ, but since we have come into the church in the Lord's recovery, we definitely see the Son of Man walking in the midst of the local churches. As to those who say, "We want Christ but not the church," the more they speak, the emptier they become. In the church we say, "We want the church!" Why do we want the church?

Because Christ is in the church. If we really care for Christ, we must care for the church. We can compare this to the way we drink water. If we say that we want water but not the cup, we cannot drink, because without the cup, there is no water.

In April 1957 several brothers who came from England and Denmark greatly appraised the audience attending a big conference held in Taipei. One elderly brother said that he had never seen such an audience in his whole life of service to the Lord. However, after a period of time he tried to put down the church. Those brothers stayed among us for eight weeks, and they very much appreciated Chinese tea. One day, we sat down to have some tea in the workers' house, and while we were enjoying the tea, we seized the opportunity to speak. To be sure, I knew what they were thinking within themselves. They thought that we were good in everything but regrettably had a "fly in the ointment," that is, the matter of the church. However, they did not dare to speak out or openly oppose. Therefore, that day in the workers' house, while we were drinking tea, I seized the opportunity to say, "You came here and really appreciate our tea, but unfortunately I have discovered that you are trying to break our teacups and our teapot." Furthermore, I said, "May I ask you, if you break our teapot and teacups, how can we serve the tea? There could be no tea." They looked at each other and understood in their heart. Nevertheless, after that time, a small number of younger co-workers were affected by them and began to shout the slogan: "We want Christ but not the church." This was twenty years ago, and there is no way to deny the fact of what has happened to them. Twenty years of history proves to us that those who want Christ but not the church are finished; they are through and have nothing.

Of course, we do not mean that we "drink the teapot but not the tea." The reason we want the "teapot" is that we want to "drink tea." When I drink tea at home, I am very particular about the teapot and the teacup. I may spend many dollars to buy the teapot but only five dollars to buy the tea. May I ask, do you spend more money on the teapot or on the tea? We have been fighting the battle for more than twenty years. Today we are still fighting; the battle is not over Christ but over the church. The focus of the dispute is not Christ but the church. Twenty years' history proves that those who want only Christ but not the church are doomed to be finished. They care only for the tea but do not care for the teapot. However, I care for both the tea and the teapot. The Bible does not stop at Exodus; rather, it goes on all the way to Revelation. At the end of Revelation there is a huge, universal "teapot" called the New Jerusalem. This is a great and unique "teapot." The divine revelation does not stop at Exodus or Zechariah but goes all the way to Revelation.

THE LAMPSTAND, JEHOVAH, THE LAMB, AND THE STONE

Now let us consider again what the golden lampstand is. We have seen that the golden lampstand is the Triune God. The Father is the substance, the Son is the form, and the Spirit is the expression. All those who have seen the light will say, "Hallelujah, the golden lampstand is the Triune God!" Now I would like to point out a few more matters. First, the Bible says that there are seven lamps on the golden lampstand, and the book of Zechariah tells us that the seven lamps are the seven eyes of Jehovah. The seven eyes are equal to the seven lamps. Who, then, is Jehovah? Jehovah is equal to the lampstand. The lampstand with the seven lamps is Jehovah with the seven eyes. This is very clear. The seven lamps are the seven eyes; hence, the lampstand is Jehovah.

Second, these seven eyes are the seven eyes of the Lamb (Rev. 5:6). Originally there was the lampstand; then there was a progression from the lampstand to Jehovah and another progression from Jehovah to the Lamb. This tells us that the lampstand is Jehovah, that Jehovah is the Lamb, that the seven lamps on the lampstand are the seven eyes of Jehovah, and that the seven eyes of Jehovah are the seven eyes of the Lamb. Moreover, Zechariah 3:9 says that these seven eyes are also the seven eyes of the stone; therefore, this stone is equal to the Lamb. The lampstand is equal to Jehovah, Jehovah is equal to the Lamb, and the Lamb is equal to the stone. These four are one. The seven lamps of the lampstand are the seven eyes of Jehovah; the seven eyes of Jehovah are the seven eyes of the Lamb; and the seven eyes of the Lamb are the seven eyes of the stone.

Do not consider this to be simple. I do not know why our God did not present these things in a simpler way when He inspired the writing of the Holy Scriptures! More than twenty years ago when I studied these items—the lampstand, Jehovah, the Lamb, and the stone—I had a very hard time with them. Today, however, I have found the way for you. If I had not found the way for you, then even after reading Exodus 25, Zechariah 3 and 4, and Revelation 1, 4, and 5 for a whole day, you would not be able to come to a proper conclusion. What are these four matters? They are the lampstand, Jehovah, the Lamb, and the stone. Now we will see three other matters: the seven lamps, the seven eyes, and the seven Spirits.

THE SEVEN LAMPS, THE SEVEN EYES, AND THE SEVEN SPIRITS

The seven lamps are the seven eyes, the seven eyes are the seven Spirits, and the seven Spirits are the seven lamps. We can keep going in a circle! What, then, do the lamps, the eyes, and the Spirits mean? Furthermore, how can the lamps be the eyes, the eyes be the Spirits, and the Spirits be the lamps? Some may say, "The seven lamps shine, the seven eyes infuse, and the seven Spirits saturate." This sounds logical, but it is still not complete. We may ask further, "How can the lampstand be Jehovah, Jehovah be the Lamb, and the Lamb be the stone?"

These truths have been buried in the Bible for centuries. Even those in the best theological schools, when reading these things, try to disregard them. They say, "Do not try to take care of so many things. Some portions in the Bible are very difficult to understand, and we should only take care of what we can understand." Eventually, many only care for John 3:16 and 1 Timothy 1:15. If we ask the theologians and study all their expository books, we cannot find anything that tells us that the lampstand is the Triune God. There is also nothing that tells us that the lampstand in Exodus emphasizes Christ, the lampstand in Zechariah emphasizes the Spirit, and the lampstands in Revelation are the churches. Hence, many Christians today do not highly regard the church because they do not have this light and revelation. We may illustrate this in the following way: I once bought a very good watch, which came in a nice-looking box. When one of my children saw the package, he did not care about the watch but asked for the box. He saw that the box was very attractive, and he appreciated the box; that was the extent of his "vision" and "revelation." Actually, that was his foolish vision and low revelation. I was wise; I kept the watch in my pocket and gave him the box because I had the insight to see what was valuable.

One day after I gave a message in Houston, Texas, a married woman came to me and said, "Brother Lee, your message was very good, but why do you speak only about the church life and not the family life?" I replied, "There are enough people speaking about the family life, so there is no need for me to speak about it. Because no one speaks about the church life, I have to make up the lack and speak specifically about the church life." I continued, "Seriously speaking, which is more precious, the church life or the family life? Which is high and which is low? Which is weighty and which is light?" I kept speaking and eventually I said, "If you do not have a proper church life, it will be hard for you to have a proper family life." That woman was separated from her husband, so she was hoping that I would say something about the family life to help them be reconciled. Actually, she did not realize that the reason for their separation was that they did not have the church life. I do not believe that any family who practices the church life will have a separation. We can boast and say that today in the practical church life there is no divorce or separation! After a quarrel, a husband will first blame himself, confess his sins, shed tears, and then go to his wife to say, "I am sorry; please forgive me. The church life compels me to confess and apologize." Therefore, I said to that woman, "Today you need the church life. I came here because I have been commissioned by the Lord to tell you that you need the church life."

THE GOLDEN LAMPSTAND BEING FOR THE CHURCH

All these precious truths are in the Bible, but because we are too shallow, we have not seen them or entered into them.

The golden lampstand is ultimately not for Christ or for the Spirit but for the church. Where does the church come from? The church comes from Christ with the Spirit. Never forget that Christ with the Spirit is the church.

The name Jesus means "Jehovah the Savior," that is, "Jehovah as our salvation." Therefore, this Jehovah is the Lamb. John 1:29 says, "Behold, the Lamb of God." Who is this Lamb? This Lamb is Jehovah the Savior, God who was incarnated to bear our iniquities in His flesh. He is our Jehovah-Lamb. He is the eternal God who came to be our Redeemer. Therefore, the eyes of Jehovah are the eyes of the Lamb. Furthermore, this Lamb not only died on the cross to bear our sins but also resurrected from the dead. In His resurrection He became the stone. How do we know this? It is not easy to explain. For this purpose we need to read Acts 3 and 4. In Acts 3:15 Peter preached the gospel, saying, "The Author of life you killed, whom God has raised from the dead." Then in 4:11 he said, "This is the stone which was considered as nothing by you, the builders, which has become the head of the corner." When did Christ become the head of the corner? It was in resurrection. The Jews considered Jesus the Nazarene as a small stone that did not deserve their attention, so they cast Him aside, even cast Him into the tomb. However, God opened the grave and brought that small stone out of the tomb and made it the first, the head, of the corner. On this stone are seven eyes. This stone is the Lamb, the Lamb is Jehovah, and Jehovah is the golden lampstand. This is not simple.

What does this all mean? This tells us that the eternal God became flesh to be the Lamb who bore our sins and redeemed us by His death, and then He was resurrected to become a stone. The stone is the lampstand, and the lampstand is the stone. We all know that the lampstand is for giving light and for shining and that the stone is for the building of God's eternal dwelling place. The first time the lampstand is spoken of in the Bible is for the building of the tabernacle. God's building can never come into being without the lampstand. If there is no lampstand, there is no building of God. The first building of God was the tabernacle, within which was the lampstand, and later in the temple there was also the golden lampstand. Still later, the temple was destroyed, and in the restoration and rebuilding of the temple in Zechariah 4, the lampstand reappeared. Thus, in God's building there is always the lampstand. On the one hand, Zechariah 3 and 4 speak of the lampstand, and on the other hand, they speak of the stone. Upon the lampstand are seven lamps, and upon the stone are seven eyes, which are the seven eyes of Jehovah. This proves that the stone is Jehovah. The seven eyes of Jehovah are the seven eyes of the stone. Is not this tantamount to saying that Jehovah is the stone? The resurrected Christ is Jehovah, but now Jehovah is a stone, and this stone is for the building of God's dwelling place. In Zechariah 4 He is for the restoration, the rebuilding, of the temple, whereas in Revelation 1 He is for the building of the church. Revelation deals with God's building, which begins with the church and reaches the New Jerusalem as its eternal goal. This building altogether hinges on Christ as the living stone.

Dear brothers and sisters, when we put all these things together, we can see a picture that is better than a thousand words. When we look at these things as a whole, we know what the church is. What is the church? Jehovah became the redeeming Lamb who died and resurrected to become the building stone; this building stone is the lampstand with seven eyes, seven Spirits, and seven lamps to produce the church. This golden lampstand is the church. This lampstand-church, or church-lampstand, is not so simple. In it there is Jehovah, there is the redeeming Lamb, and there is the resurrected stone. The lampstand is here, the seven lamps are here, and the seven Spirits are here; all these items are present.

NEEDING TO GO FORTH TO EVERY PLACE
TO BEAR THE TESTIMONY OF THE CHURCH

Now we can see what the church is. It is the church, not Christianity, that must go to bear the testimony in every place. When I speak about this, a fire is ignited within me. I want to stir you up so that you will go out to preach the gospel of the glorious church and bear the testimony of the church. Every city, town, village, and hamlet on the island of Taiwan needs this testimony. I am very happy in my visit at this time because I see that so many young people are burning with love for the Lord and bearing the responsibility for the service in this conference. Today, however, I want to stir you up to go forth. You need to go through the entire island of Taiwan and establish a church in every place. This is not to establish Christianity but to establish the church in the Lord's recovery.

I want to disturb your "nests" so that from this day on you can no longer have a peaceful life; rather, you need to go out and preach the gospel. "Go therefore and disciple all the nations, baptizing them into the name of the Father and of the Son and of the Holy Spirit" (Matt. 28:19). We say Amen! You should go first through the entire island of Taiwan and then to Southeast Asia. This age is yours; you should not preach the low gospel, a gospel merely for people to be forgiven of their sins and for their souls to be saved. Rather, you should preach the gospel of the glorious church. Our Bridegroom will come, but where is the bride? There must be churches raised up in every locality on earth. Only the proper church can be His bride.

Today this is the work that the Lord is doing in the United States, Europe, and South America. This is why nearly the whole of Christianity in Europe and America is opposing us. Today the Lord needs the testimony of the lampstand; He needs the churches as the lampstands in every locality. It does not matter whether our number is big or small; what matters are the brightness of the lamps and the shining of the gold. The hope of such a testimony rests on you who are the young generation. We thank the Lord that from 1948 to this day His testimony has been in Taipei for twenty-nine years. Many of you who are the working young people are the crystallization of this testimony of twenty-nine years. If you do not rise up, this testimony will not have much future or prospect. Therefore, today I hope that your eyes will be opened to see that in the Bible what the Lord desires to have ultimately is the lampstand with Christ, full of the Spirit, with the shining of the lamps and the gold, bearing the testimony for the Lord. Every city, every town, and every village on the whole island of Taiwan must have such a testimony. One place may have thirty people meeting together, another forty, another twenty,

and still another fifty. In every locality there must be a lampstand. You have heard enough, eaten enough, and enjoyed
enough; today you should accept such a commission.

CHAPTER THREE

CHRIST AS THE TOPSTONE
FOR GOD'S BUILDING

Scripture Reading: Zech. 3:9; 4:7; Acts 4:10-12; John 1:42; Matt. 16:18; 1 Pet. 2:4-5; 1 Cor. 3:12; Rev. 21:11, 18-19a

THE CHURCH BEING THE REPRINT
OF THE SPIRIT WITH CHRIST

I hope that every one of us can have a clear vision of the church being the reprint of the Spirit with Christ. The church is a reprint, a reproduction. This has been missed in today's Christianity. Christianity is merely a religion and a human organization; it is not the reprint of the Spirit with Christ. The Lord's recovery today is the recovery of the church as the reprint of the Spirit with Christ. For this reason we have a burden that not only in one locality or in one country but in every locality and in every country there could be a living testimony of the church. This does not depend on having a big number or a small number of people; rather, it depends on having some saints who meet together in the Lord's name, in the Lord's person, as Christ's reprint, Christ's reproduction.

Let us consider what the reprint of the Spirit with Christ really means. We all know what a reprint is. If we have an article that has been typeset, with every word correct and lacking nothing, all that is needed is to reprint the original on many sheets of paper. One original can be reproduced on thousands of sheets of paper. This is the meaning of a reprint. Christ is one and the Spirit is one, but the Spirit with Christ wants to reprint Christ onto the church. Whatever is in the original is also in every reprint, without "different words" or "missing punctuation." This is the church. The church is the reprint of Christ; it is a "printed book" of the Spirit with Christ.

What, then, is the content of this reprint? The revelation in the Bible concerning this matter is not simple. Because it is not simple, the Bible uses figures to make it clear. For example, the tabernacle as a type of God's dwelling place involves a great deal; if we do not have a picture but only use words, we cannot explain it thoroughly and clearly. Therefore, in His wisdom God gave us the tabernacle as a picture. When we look at this picture, spontaneously we understand what God's dwelling place is. This kind of representation is clearer than a thousand words. The church being the reprint of the Spirit with Christ cannot be clearly explained even with thousands of words. Therefore, there is a symbol in the Bible to show it, yet the symbol itself is not easy to understand. We have seen that the golden lampstand apparently is simple, yet it is not simple when we really get into it.

THE LAMPSTAND, JEHOVAH, THE LAMB, AND THE STONE

In the previous chapter we mentioned four things: the lampstand, Jehovah, the Lamb, and the stone. We have proved that the lampstand is Jehovah, Jehovah is the Lamb, and the Lamb is the stone. The key to our proof is the seven lamps. These seven lamps are the seven eyes, and the seven eyes are the seven Spirits. The seven lamps of the lampstand are the seven eyes of Jehovah (Zech. 4:2, 10); naturally, this shows that the lampstand is Jehovah. Jehovah with seven eyes equals the lampstand with seven lamps. The Bible also says that the seven eyes of Jehovah are the seven eyes of the Lamb (Rev. 5:6). Hence, this also proves that Jehovah is equal to the Lamb and the Lamb is equal to Jehovah. Moreover, the Bible says that the seven eyes are the seven eyes of the stone (Zech. 3:9). This proves that the stone is equal to the Lamb. Eventually, the Bible says that the seven eyes are the seven Spirits of God (Rev. 5:6). Therefore, we can say that the lampstand equals Jehovah, Jehovah equals the Lamb, the Lamb equals the stone, and the stone equals God. There are seven lamps, seven eyes, and seven Spirits. The seven lamps belong to the lampstand, and the seven eyes belong to Jehovah, the Lamb, and the stone. The seven eyes are also the seven Spirits of God. If we put these few passages of the Bible together, we can definitely see that the seven lamps are the seven eyes, and the seven eyes are the seven Spirits. Based on this, the lampstand is Jehovah, Jehovah is the Lamb, the Lamb is the stone, and the stone is God. This kind of saying may prick the ears of theologians. They may ask, "How can you say that the lampstand is Jehovah and that the stone is God? What kind of theology is this?" This is the authentic theology in the Bible. Many theologians do not know the Bible; mostly they know traditional theology. They do not see God's direct revelation, the divine word. If, for example, the Lord Jesus had not said with His own mouth that "the stone which the builders rejected, this has become the head of the corner" (Matt. 21:42), I am convinced that not one theologian would be willing to make such a statement. Even though the Lord Jesus did say this, today's theologians do not speak much about it because they do not understand it clearly. They do not know how the Lord Jesus can be a stone and how this stone can be the stone which was cut out without hands to smash the great image in Nebuchadnezzar's dream and eventually become a great mountain to fill the whole earth (Dan. 2:31-35).

Jehovah—
God in His Relationship with Man

Let us forget about the theologians and come back to the Bible. The Bible says that this lampstand is Jehovah, Jehovah is the Lamb, the Lamb is the stone, and the stone is God. Dear brothers and sisters, we must see these matters clearly if we want to know the church. We should not forget that the lampstand is the Triune God. How, then, is the lampstand Jehovah? We need to be clear that in the Bible the title *Jehovah* is used specifically concerning God in His contact with man, His relationship with man. In Genesis 1, a chapter on God's creation, *Jehovah* is not used even once, but *God* is used repeatedly. God is the Creator. It is not until chapter 2, concerning God's relationship with man, that the title *Jehovah* is introduced. In the name Jesus, *Je-* refers to Jehovah, and *-sus* denotes the Savior or salvation. The name Jesus means "Jehovah being our Savior and becoming our salvation." Therefore, the name Jehovah denotes the Triune God in His contact and relationship with man. It is true that the golden lampstand is the Triune God, but this Triune God is not without a relationship with man. The Triune God has become the golden lampstand so that He may contact man and have a relationship with man. Therefore, this Triune God—the golden lampstand, Jehovah—desires to contact man and have a relationship with him.

The Lamb—
Taking Away Man's Sins

How can God have a relationship with man? How can He contact man? Man is sinful, but God is sinless; man is evil, but God is holy. It is not possible for that which is sinless to have a relationship with that which is sinful, and it is not permissible for that which is holy to contact that which is common. In other words, there is no possibility for the Triune God to have a relationship with sinful man unless there is the shedding of blood by the Lamb, for without the shedding of blood there is no forgiveness of sins. Therefore, it is not enough to have only Jehovah; Jehovah had to become Jesus as the Lamb.

The Stone—
for the Building of God's Dwelling Place

Here we see a progression. For the Triune God to have contact with man, He must be Jehovah; for Jehovah to have contact with man, He must be the Lamb to take away our sins. However, His being the Lamb is not the goal; it is the procedure. The taking away of man's sins is the procedure, but the goal is the building of God's eternal dwelling place. Therefore, after the Lamb there is the stone, and this stone is related to the Lamb. The Lamb takes away man's sins, and the stone has been engraved (Zech. 3:9). Because He has been engraved, the iniquities of God's people are removed in one day. At what point did God engrave the stone? It was on the cross. The Lord's death on the cross, that is, His suffering on the cross, was God's engraving. On the cross God engraved the Lord Jesus, referring to the death, the slaying, the shedding of blood, of the Lamb, and that engraving removed the iniquities of the world and of God's people in one day. Thus, the Lamb and the stone are connected. The Lamb is for redemption and the stone is for building; thus, redemption is joined to building. The result of this progression—the lampstand, Jehovah, the Lamb, and the stone—is God Himself.

THE FOUNDATION STONE,
THE CORNERSTONE, AND THE TOPSTONE

I hope these matters are clear. Here, we will give more time not to the lampstand, Jehovah, or the Lamb, but to the stone. I do not believe that among today's Christians there are many messages given concerning the stone. Zechariah 3 says that Jehovah set a stone before Joshua the high priest, and upon that stone were seven eyes. Then chapter 4 says that Zerubbabel would bring forth a stone as the topstone of the temple. Joshua was the priest, and Zerubbabel as a descendant of David represents the royal family, the royal authority. The priesthood and the kingship joined together to bring forth the stone. The stone in 3:9 is the stone in 4:7. The stone in 3:9 has seven eyes, and the stone in 4:7 is a topstone.

The Jews built their houses mainly with three kinds of stones: the foundation stone, the cornerstone, and the topstone as the covering of the house. The housetop was flat, and on the flat surface was a topstone. First there was the foundation stone, then there was the cornerstone to join the walls together, and then there was the topstone above. When the topstone was placed on the housetop, the building of the house was completed. The Bible tells us that the Lord Jesus is the foundation stone, the cornerstone, and the topstone of God's building. When the topstone is set, God's building will be completed. Upon the topstone are seven eyes, just as on the golden lampstand the seven lamps are not at its base or at its midsection but on its top part. This means that the Lord Jesus as the material for God's building has seven eyes upon Him, not as the foundation stone or the cornerstone but as the topstone.

THE PROCESS FOR BECOMING THE TOPSTONE—
DEATH AND RESURRECTION

A stone goes through a considerable process to arrive at the stage of being a topstone. This process implies death and resurrection. In Matthew 21:42 the Lord Jesus told the Jews that the stone which they rejected was made by God to be the cornerstone. In Acts 4:10-12, after the Lord's resurrection, Peter preached the gospel to the Jews, telling them that they needed to know that Jesus Christ, the Nazarene whom they crucified, had been raised from the dead and that the stone which they, the builders, rejected had been made the cornerstone by God.

While the Lord Jesus was on the earth before He was killed, He was persecuted and rejected by the Jews. At that time He was a stone that had not been resurrected. He was a stone that had not passed through the procedure, being without resurrection. At that time people could not see much glory upon Him; they only saw a small stone from Nazareth. The Jews despised this stone; they showed no respect to this stone, considering it merely a small stone from Nazareth of Galilee. Hence, they cast it away and even buried it in a tomb. After such a casting away and burial, God came in to bring the stone out of the tomb. Before His crucifixion He was a small Nazarene. The Bible says that "He has no attracting form nor majesty that we should look upon Him, / Nor beautiful appearance that we should desire Him" (Isa. 53:2b). However, after He was raised from the dead, He became the glorious Son of Man. This means that after His death and resurrection, He became the first stone in resurrection. When He was cast away, He was a small stone from Nazareth, but after His resurrection from the dead, He was transformed into a condition like that of His transfiguration on the mountain, in which His entire being was transfigured, His face shone like the sun, and His garments became as white as the light. He no longer looked like a Nazarene who had no attracting form nor majesty. When the Lord was transfigured on the mountain, Peter said, "It is good for us to be here" (Matt. 17:4). That was a miniature of the Lord Jesus' resurrection. The Lord Jesus' resurrection from the dead was the transfiguration of His whole being. In other

words, that small stone from Nazareth became a precious
stone, exceedingly glorious and bright.

CLAY, STONE, AND PRECIOUS STONE

First we see the golden lampstand and then the stone. This
sequence—the golden lampstand, Jehovah, the Lamb, and the
stone—is very meaningful. Gold is not something transformed, but precious stones are something transformed. The
more they are transformed, the more glorious and precious
they become. Gold denotes the Lord's divinity, whereas the
stone denotes His humanity. According to His divinity, He
is gold; according to His humanity, He is stone. His divinity is
unchangeable, but His humanity, which was not that glorious
or bright as a Nazarene before His death, became glorious, bril-
liant, and resplendent like a precious stone.

Let us repeat, using the stone as a figure: When He was
in the flesh, He was a small stone from Nazareth, having
no splendor or brilliance. Therefore, the Jews looked down
upon Him and cast Him aside. They counted Him as nothing,
considering that nothing good could come from Nazareth.
Hence, they cast Him aside and buried Him in the tomb, but
God resurrected Him. This stone from Nazareth was changed,
but His divinity was not changed. What, then, was changed?
His humanity was changed. The eternal God did not change,
but Jesus the Nazarene was changed. The divine nature is unchanged, just as pure gold cannot change, but the humanity
that He had put on was changed.

Originally, we were not stones but clay. Thank the Lord,
one day we were saved, and the pure gold came into us. John
1:12 says, "As many as received Him, to them He gave the
authority to become children of God, to those who believe into
His name." Since we have become the children of God, within
us is the divine nature, which is pure gold. Within us we all
have a portion of the ever-unchanging pure gold. However, we
ourselves are clay. The record in John 1:42 tells us that when
Peter was brought before the Lord, the Lord immediately
changed his name. Originally, he was called Simon, but the
Lord said, "You shall be called Cephas." *Cephas* being inter-
preted is *a stone;* hence, "You are a stone." I believe at that

moment Peter became a stone, but I also believe he was not yet a precious stone. The Peter in the Gospels was not precious at all. On the one hand, I like him, because my disposition is much like his: straightforward and quick. On the other hand, I am a little disgusted with him because he was not precious and was barely even a stone. However, the New Jerusalem has a foundation of twelve layers of precious stones, one of which is Peter. In Revelation 21 the stone that is called Peter is no longer an ordinary stone but a precious stone. He was changed. When he came to see the Lord, the clay was changed by the Lord to a stone. After following the Lord for many years, this stone became a precious stone.

Matthew 16 tells us that one day the Lord Jesus brought His disciples into the parts of Caesarea Philippi. The sky there was clear, unlike in Jerusalem where the religious atmosphere was thick and dense. It was there in Caesarea Philippi that the Lord asked them, "Who do you say that I am?" Simon Peter answered and said, "You are the Christ, the Son of the living God." The Lord Jesus said, "You are Peter," that is, "You are a stone" (vv. 15-16, 18). That was to remind him once again that he was a stone, and upon the rock of that revelation the Lord would build His church. Originally, Peter was clay, but he became a stone by knowing the Lord. Later, in his first Epistle, Peter said that the Lord is a living stone and we come to Him also as living stones. Just as He is a living stone, so also we are living stones. As living stones, we are being built up as a spiritual house, a holy priesthood.

Today some in Christianity also claim that they are the church. I believe that in their mind they consider that as long as there is a group of people who have been baptized in the name of Jesus and have formed a Christian organization, that is the "church." However, our eyes must be opened to see that this is not the church. What is the church? The church is a group of muddy people, people of clay, into whom a new nature has entered, by a new birth, to make them people of stone. These people of stone, however, still have to become people of precious stones.

I can see that many of the young brothers and sisters have a seeking heart. Consider this: Were you clay before you were saved? Yes, you were really clay, but one day you were saved, and the pure gold came into you, but others could not see much stone in you. Perhaps a little transformation began in you with a tiny amount of stone, but it was hardly noticeable. Gradually, however, others can see a little stone. A few years ago when I came to Taiwan, I saw that some of the "small stones" were not bad, but neither were they precious. However, at this time, I notice that at least some among the young people are beginning to become precious. This means that others can see in them not only stone but also precious stone.

BUILDING THE CHURCH WITH PRECIOUS STONES

In 1 Corinthians 3:12 Paul says that we should build upon Christ as the foundation with gold, silver, and precious stones. He speaks not merely of stones but of precious stones. We must see that the ultimate consummation of the church is the New Jerusalem. In the New Jerusalem there is no clay, and there are not even stones. The New Jerusalem only has precious stones. Merely to be a stone is not enough; the stone must be precious. Do not consider this matter as mere doctrine. The Lord needs a church of precious stones today. The Lord does not want wood, grass, and stubble; what He wants is gold, silver, and precious stones.

If we carefully look at the New Jerusalem, we will see that the pure gold is mostly not used for the building; rather, it is for the base of the city. Revelation 21 tells us that the street of the city is pure gold (v. 21b). This does not mean that the street is paved with gold. Instead, it means that the entire base of the New Jerusalem is a gold mountain. The entire mountain is pure gold. Hence, strictly speaking, gold is not for the building. What, then, is used for the building? Precious stones are used. The building's main emphasis is on the walls, which are built with precious stones. You have been saved and I also have been saved, so we all have pure gold in us. The brothers and sisters who have been saved in the denominations also have pure gold in them. Furthermore, even in the Catholic Church, as long as people have been genuinely saved, they also have pure gold in them. However, we must see that those who are in the Catholic Church and in the Protestant denominations are not being built up with those who love the Lord, because the building depends not on the gold but on the precious stones.

We have been saved and have the gold in us. It is possible for the element of gold in us to increase because the element of God increases. This is not transformation but addition. However, whether we are clay, just a stone, or a precious stone is not a matter of addition but a matter of transformation. The gold within us needs to increase, while as a lump of clay and a piece of stone, we need to be transformed. Today Christians in general do not have the reality of the church. They are the church in name but not in reality. Where is the reality of the church? The reality of the church is in the gold and precious stones. The gold needs to increase, and the stones need to be transformed.

The ultimate aggregate of the golden lampstand is the church, and the church is the reprint of the golden lampstand. The golden lampstand is first the pure gold and then the precious stones. Today's church must first have the pure gold and then have the precious stones. Pure gold is very much lacking among Christians. Today we may meet a denominational Christian, and although he has been saved, it may take more than three hours to touch a tiny fragment of pure gold in him. Unless we contact him for a longer time, we are not even sure whether he has been saved, regenerated, or has God's life. How can that small "chip" of gold be sufficient for the church and the New Jerusalem? It is not possible. However, sometimes when I visit a church in the Lord's recovery, although I see the pure gold, I do not see much stone. Rather, I see much clay, even mire. Without stones, how can the church be built? I want to speak a frank word to you, brothers and sisters: We should be conscious to not go on in this way year after year. We need to bring forth the stones and the precious stones. We must not only wash away the mud but also transform the clay into stone. The mud should be washed away, but the clay should be transformed. We must see that the church is first a lampstand, then a stone, and then a precious stone.

DOING THE WORK OF PRECIOUS STONES

Today the Lord has sent me neither to flatter nor to offend

people. Rather, He has sent me to minister life to others and burn them with the seven lamps of fire to dry up the mud, turn the clay into stones, and turn the stones into precious stones. We must not do an ambiguous work with great "mounds of clay" having no stones or precious stones in sight. I hope that the young generation among us will rise up and go out. What the Lord wants today is the church. I have no burden to come back to Taiwan to give a few messages. I did not come back at this time to make your days peaceful. For so many years we have been giving messages every week, yet not one stone has been brought forth. Should we still give messages? Now is not the time for us to give messages; what we need today is to wash away the mud and transform the clay into stones and the stones into precious stones. The pure gold needs to increase, the clay needs to be transformed, and even the stones need to be transformed into precious stones.

If anyone builds upon the foundation, let him take heed how he builds, whether it is with gold, silver, and precious stones or with wood, grass, and stubble. If we build with wood, grass, and stubble, the more work we do, the more fuel for fire we have; we would be better off doing less. We need to work out the precious stones. We are not here to merely drift along. We do not have time for this! The Lord is very near. We should bear a burden. If we have mud, we must empty it and dry it up; if we have clay, we must transform it into stones and precious stones. Thank the Lord that the lampstand is first pure gold and then a stone. Please remember that when we come to the stone, it is not merely a matter of redemption. The matter of redemption is with the Lamb. When we come to the stone, it is a matter of the topstone. The stone has been placed on the top of the temple, and the building has been completed. Therefore, everyone can shout, "Grace, grace to the stone!" (Zech. 4:7). Only upon this stone can there be grace.

We need to come back to the Lord, for the time is short. Today in the Lord's recovery the light has been intensified, so it is not possible for anyone to drift along blindly. Everyone's eyes are clear. To do something just to get by is completely worthless, and to go through the motions without sincerity is valueless. We must do the work of precious stones. We need to lead others to be saved, but that is not enough. We must see that our work is also to inject life into people, injection by injection, that the clay may become stones and the stones may become precious stones. This is the building that the Lord is after today.

CHAPTER FOUR

THE SEVEN BURNING LAMPS OF FIRE
FOR GOD'S MOVE

Scripture Reading: Exo. 25:37; 27:20-21; 30:7-8; Rev. 4:5; 1:4;
Psa. 73:17

We have looked at a number of aspects of the golden lampstand. We have seen the Triune God, God's relationship with man, the Lamb's redemption, Christ as God's building material, and God Himself. If we lack sufficient knowledge of these matters, we will never see the church clearly. If we would have a thorough understanding of the church, we have to realize that the church involves the Triune God, God's relationship with man, Christ's redemption, and God's building. Eventually, everything is God Himself.

The children of God throughout the ages have only had a one-sided and fragmented understanding concerning the church. They do not have the thorough light from God to see that the church is entirely a matter of the golden lampstand. From the past up until the present, the understanding of many Christians, theologians, and Bible teachers concerning the golden lampstand only goes as far as the revelation concerning Christ. They only know that the golden lampstand is Christ. They do not go a step further to Zechariah to see that the golden lampstand also refers to the Holy Spirit. Neither do they enter into Revelation to see that the final destination of the lampstand is the church. Strictly speaking, the golden lampstand is a testimony of God in the universe, which begins with Christ, passes through the Spirit, and reaches the church. There are quite a number of items involved that are also important: the Triune God, God's relationship with man (indicated by the name *Jehovah*), Christ's redemption, and God's building. All these items are included in this testimony, and eventually, there is God Himself as all in all. God is His own testimony, and God's testimony is just He Himself. We should never forget this sequence: the golden lampstand, Jehovah, the Lamb, the stone, and God Himself.

THE SEVEN LAMPS OF THE LAMPSTAND BEING THE SEVEN LAMPS BEFORE THE THRONE OF GOD

Now we want to see the seven lamps, which are a crucial item of the golden lampstand. The main emphasis of the golden lampstand is its shining, and the shining depends on the seven lamps. This matter is not simple. If we only look at Exodus 25, we cannot see much. We can only see the record of a golden lampstand upon which are seven shining lamps. Its stem is in the center with six branches coming out of its two sides, three on each side, and the branches on the two sides shine toward each other.

Revelation 1:4 says, "From Him who is and who was and who is coming, and from the seven Spirits who are before His throne." God's throne is present at the very beginning of Revelation. In the universe God has a center of administration, which is His throne. Revelation 4:5 says that lightnings and voices and thunders come forth out of the throne. Lightnings, voices, and thunders are a sign, a symbol, signifying that God is administering and moving from His throne to execute His eternal policy. The throne of God is the center of His administration, and upon His throne He executes His eternal policy and eternal purpose. Here, God has His move, administration, management, economy, and eternal operation. Verse 5 also says that "the seven Spirits of God" are "seven lamps of fire burning before the throne." The speaking in the Bible is very economical, and there are no wasted words. The seven lamps on the golden lampstand are the seven lamps of fire before the throne of God. This signifies that the seven lamps are absolutely related to God's administration, economy, and move. God's move depends on these seven lamps.

THE TABERNACLE HAVING
THE LIGHT ONLY OF THE LAMPSTAND

We must spend some time here. The lampstand was placed in the tabernacle, and in the tabernacle there was no door or window. There was no opening above or below, on the left or on the right, or at the front or at the back of the tabernacle. There was one opening at the entrance to the tabernacle, but it was fully concealed by the veil. For anyone today to build a house without windows or doors would be a great folly. Yet, wonderfully, God built a dwelling place, the tabernacle, without windows or doors; only a curtain hung at the entrance as a veil, which hid the light. Therefore, in the tabernacle it was dark, having neither sunlight nor moonlight. However, in the Holy Place there was a golden lampstand, which had not only one lamp but seven lamps shining and illuminating.

Both the sunlight and the moonlight are natural light for us to observe natural things, such as mountains, rivers, flowers, grass, trees, and wild beasts. However, natural light cannot help us to know God's administration, God's economy, and God's eternal purpose. To know God's administration and economy, we must have the light of the golden lampstand. When we enter into the realm of God's presence, there is no light without the golden lampstand. Outside the realm of God's presence, we have sunlight and moonlight, and we have the natural view, but we can never have the view of God's economy and administration. A university professor may have obtained three doctoral degrees and may have taught for thirty years. Whenever science, literature, or philosophy are mentioned, his "moon" grows bigger and his "sun" radiates the light of his knowledge. Nevertheless, his light is "sunlight" and "moonlight," that is, natural light. He can understand science, literature, and philosophy, but when he comes to the realm of God's presence, his eyes are darkened; he knows nothing whatsoever about God's administration and God's economy—they are foreign to him. In contrast, some of the young people have only been in the church for two or three years, yet they know God's eternal economy. In other words, they know the divine economics. This is not a small matter. University professors only know the things within their field of research, but when they come into the realm of God's presence, their eyes are completely darkened. We, however, know God's economy, God's administration, and the dispensations in God's administration.

Do not forget that in the realm of God's presence, the light is neither sunlight nor moonlight but the light of the golden lampstand. The light of the golden lampstand is the light of God's administration. Even though the tabernacle is small, the propitiation place within it is the throne of God. God's throne is in the tabernacle, and before the throne are the seven bright burning lamps. When we enter into the tabernacle, we cannot do anything without these seven bright lamps, because without them, we are not able to see anything. When a priest entered into the tabernacle, his actions were dependent upon the shining of these seven bright lamps. The light of the seven bright lamps dictated all the actions of the priests in the tabernacle. This is the way of God's administration, government, and economy.

THE LIGHT OF THE LAMPSTAND
ENABLING MAN TO UNDERSTAND
GOD'S ADMINISTRATION AND ECONOMY

We must be deeply impressed that the golden lampstand, as well as the tabernacle itself, is the church. This means that the shining of the church is in the church. Outside the church is the light of the "sun" and the "moon" but not the light of the golden lampstand. Outside the church is the natural view but not the light of revelation that shines out of God's lampstand. For this reason, not only non-Christians but even many Christians do not know what God's economy, God's administration, is. This is because they are not in the Holy Place; they are not before the throne of God, and they are not under the shining of the seven lamps. The shining of the seven lamps is in the Holy Place. I repeat: The golden lampstand is the church, and the tabernacle is also the church. This means that the light of the lampstand is in the church.

Let me give a small testimony. I was saved in old Christianity. At that time all that I was taught was that I was a sinner and that I could go to heaven by believing in the Lord. Later,

I was brought to the Brethren to learn the Bible. I came to have much knowledge concerning the Bible, but I knew nothing about God's economy, God's administration. The Brethren did not have this light. Sometimes they taught that we have to obey God's will in every matter. However, what they meant by this was that children must try their best to seek God's will so that they may know how to obey their parents. When they are about to enter high school, they have to seek God's will again. There may be many high schools in their city, so they must pray to attend the one of His will. Eventually, when they arrive at the marrying age, they must pray, "O Lord, I ask that You may make it clear to me which one is the partner You are giving me. Is she from the Lee, the Chang, the Wang, or the Liu family?" They also taught me that even when I go to buy a pair of shoes, I have to pray, "O Lord, do You want me to get a pair of shoes made of fabric or of leather? What sort of shoes do You want me to wear according to Your will?" At that time I thought that it was very good and meaningful to pray to ask God concerning His intention when choosing a school, selecting a mate, and even buying a pair of shoes. Thank the Lord, after this time He brought me to the church. The first day I came to the church, I saw light. It was not "sunlight" or "moonlight"; it was the light from the seven lamps on the golden lampstand. What I saw was not leather shoes versus fabric shoes or the Lee, Chang, Wang, or Liu family. Instead, I saw God's eternal purpose. I saw God's eternal administration and economy. This was a tremendous seeing! After I saw this, I realized that I can put on either fabric shoes or leather shoes as long as they are appropriate. It is not a matter of fabric shoes versus leather shoes; it is a matter of God's administration, God's economy.

Brothers and sisters, if you do not believe my word, leave the churches in the Lord's recovery and meet in a denomination, and try to see if you are able to stay there for half a year. I can guarantee that in that situation, the more you go to their Sunday worship service, the thicker the veils will become and the more befuddled your mind will be. You will not have even a small amount of light. In contrast, many can testify that as soon as they stepped into the church meetings, the light was shining, they became clear, and they had the realization not of wearing fabric shoes versus leather ones but of God's administration, God's economy. They realized that the throne is here and that there are seven lamps of fire burning before the throne. What kind of light is this? This is not the light of the sky, the natural light; rather, it is the light of the Holy Place.

THE LIGHT OF THE HOLY PLACE
BEING IN THE CHURCH

I hope that we will practice using the phrase *the light of the Holy Place.* The light of the golden lampstand is the light of the Holy Place, not the light of the sky, nor that of the sun, the moon, or anything natural. The light of the Holy Place is from the burning of the olive oil in the golden lampstand. The Holy Place today is the church. The church is the lampstand, and it is also the Holy Place. That the lampstand is in the Holy Place means that the church is in the church. This may seem to be a peculiar statement, but we can confirm it from our experience. In Psalm 73 the psalmist saw a situation that puzzled him and was difficult to comprehend. The more he looked at it, the more it was unclear to him; the more he analyzed it, the more it did not make sense and the more he became befuddled. Eventually, he said, "When I considered this in order to understand it, / It was a troublesome task in my sight, / Until I went into the sanctuary of God; / Then I perceived their end" (vv. 16-17). This shows us that when he went into the sanctuary, the Holy Place, he understood. Likewise, many among us can give such a testimony: "Until I came into the church, then I understood." Very often we face problems, and we remain perplexed after much pondering over them. Nevertheless, once we come to the meetings, immediately we understand. Do you have this experience? I can testify that a thousand times I am pressed, I am befuddled, I am at a loss, and I do not understand, but once I come into the meetings, I fully understand. Why is this? It is because in the Holy Place there is the shining of the seven lamps.

Today in certain places, especially in America, some people feel very unhappy when they hear us say that we are the church. In Anaheim we are the church, in Los Angeles we are the church, and in San Francisco we are the church. This saying pricks the ears of some in the denominations. They say, "Don't we worship God? Don't we believe in the Lord Jesus? Don't we have the Bible? Don't we pray? Don't we depend on the precious blood? Why are you the church and we aren't?" This is hard to argue, but whether or not we are something is not a matter of argument. I am Witness Lee, but another may say, "Only you are Witness Lee? Am I not Witness Lee also?" Even if he argues and becomes angry, I am still Witness Lee, and he is not. If one is, he is; if one is not, he is not. It is useless to argue. In the same way, denominations say that they are the church. However, once people go there, they are confused. Even if they hang a signboard outside that reads, "We are the church," once people come in, it is pitch dark and there is no light. Neither the church in Anaheim nor the church in Los Angeles has a signboard that says, "We are the church," but hundreds of people have said, "Now I understand!" once they came into these churches. Once people come to the church, they see light. As to whether or not a meeting is the church, the key factor is whether or not the lampstand is there and people see light when they meet. It is not that anyone who claims to be the church is the church; the question is whether or not people touch light when they come in.

A certain place may have a preacher who is born with sophisticated eloquence, a sonorous voice, and clear enunciation. He speaks clearly and logically and quotes copiously from the Scriptures. All these are attractive to people and are as pleasant as music to their ears. People may be very touched after listening to him, but there still may be no light, and their vision is pitch dark. However, when we come to the meetings of the church, a brother may stutter when he speaks, and he may not present matters clearly, yet even if people have a hard time listening, the light is there and it shines brightly. Eloquence is one thing, but light is another.

I trust that many of us have had this experience. When we come to the church meetings, even before the reading of the Bible, even as soon as we are seated, we are enlightened. We are clear. Not only are we clear about wearing leather shoes versus fabric shoes; we are also clear concerning the course of our whole life. Therefore, whether or not we are the church does not depend on eloquence, exalted speech, great wisdom, or learning but on whether or not the seven lamps are shining. This is not man-made light, and neither is it sunlight nor moonlight; rather, it is the light of the seven lamps on the golden lampstand in the Holy Place. Today not only ordinary Christians but even many pastors, preachers, and professors in Bible seminaries do not know what human life actually is, and they are even more unskilled concerning God's administration, God's economy. Nevertheless, I can guarantee that as long as we come into the realm of the church, all we have to do is sit in the meetings, and meeting after meeting we will become clear inwardly. We will receive a thorough understanding of human life, and we will become completely clear about God's will. We will be crystal clear about God's economy, and we will know the age that we are in today. This is due to the light in the Holy Place.

I love to use this expression, *the light in the Holy Place.* "When I considered this in order to understand it, / It was a troublesome task in my sight, / Until I went into the sanctuary of God; / Then I perceived their end." Once we go into the Holy Place, we understand. This is because in the Holy Place is the throne, the One who sits on the throne, and the presence of God, and before the throne of God is the shining of the seven burning lamps of fire. Once we enter into this realm, immediately we are clear. We know God's eternal purpose, His heart's intention, and His economy, and we also know which path we should take for the journey before us. This is due to the light in the Holy Place.

THE LIGHT OF THE LAMPSTAND BEING
BASED ON THE STRENGTH OF THE PRIESTS' SERVICE

Nevertheless, forgive me to say that sometimes, in certain local churches, the light is not bright. It is not that there is no light, but that there is only a small amount of light. In 1 Samuel 3, when Samuel ministered to Jehovah as a child before Eli, "the lamp of God had not yet gone out" (v. 3). This means that the lamp was about to go out because old Eli the priest was too weak. Exodus says that the lamps in the Holy

Place were lit by the priests. The priests had to burn the incense when they dressed the lamps in the morning and when they lit them in the evening. To burn the incense is to pray. Whether or not the lamps of a local church are bright is absolutely related to the priests' burning of incense before God. The reason that the lamps are not bright is that the service, the priesthood, and the burning of incense are absent. Although the Holy Place and the lampstand are real, the priestly ministry may be weak, like that of Eli. Today in some local churches the light in the Holy Place is not bright because the priests are too weak. Whether or not the light of the lamps is bright is absolutely related to the service of the priesthood.

Many in this conference come from different local churches. I hope that you will not care whether or not you are responsible brothers. No matter where you come from, you have responsibility placed on you. It is imperative that you go back to burn the incense and light the lamps. You must brighten up the light of the lamps in the local church so that when people come to the church, they will feel that it is full of light and that it is impossible for them to hide anything. Under the light there is no place to hide or conceal anything. Each local church should be so bright that once people enter in, all their situations are fully exposed so that they cannot help saying, "God is indeed among you, because my secrets have been thoroughly revealed under the shining of your light. This light is even more penetrating than an x-ray." The church should be this way.

The church is the Holy Place, the church is the lampstand, and the church is the lampstand in the Holy Place. Not only so, in the church there is also the priesthood for the burning of the incense. Do not say that when I speak of the priesthood, I am probably referring to the elders. No, each one of us has a share in the priesthood. We are all kings and priests, and we all have to learn to fulfill our duty of burning the incense. When we light the lamps, we have to burn the incense. Is the light bright in the local church where we are? We have to burn the incense to light the lamps. When we light the lamps at night, we have to burn the incense, and when we dress the lamps in the morning, we also have to burn the incense. This means that we have to pray at night and in the morning so that the light of God may shine brightly among us. The light should be so bright that the illumining of the light becomes God's move, His administration, His government in the universe, and His economy on earth today. This is not a small matter.

If our conference were merely a gathering of people in Christianity, this would be an exceedingly great failure. We must see, and we must be clear and realize, that this conference is the shining of the great light, and this shining is God's move, God's administration. This is the economy of God on earth today. It is very good that we see our past mistakes and failures at this time. We thank God for this. This is God's visitation upon us so that we may be able to see. However, if this is all that happens, this conference has failed. What I hope is that whether we are young or old, we all will say, "I am under the shining of the great light. In this meeting I have come to understand human life and God's eternal purpose, and I have come to know the church as God's economy." This should be the result. The issue of this conference should be that we all have been brought into the Holy Place and that in the Holy Place we all are under the shining of the light from the lampstand. Under this light we know what God's way is. Today, even though many preachers are preaching, they do not know what God's economy is. To be sure, although many Western missionaries are preaching the word abroad every day, they are puzzled within as to what God's way is, and they wonder how they should walk in order to be on God's way. Nevertheless, many can testify that when we turned to the church, we immediately saw that God's light is here, and we came to know God's economy and His way.

THE LAMPSTAND BEING WHERE THE CHURCH IS

Revelation 1 says that when John was in spirit, he heard a loud voice, saying, "What you see write in a scroll and send it to the seven churches: to Ephesus and to Smyrna and to Pergamos and to Thyatira and to Sardis and to Philadelphia and to Laodicea" (v. 11). After he heard the voice, John goes on to say, "When I turned, I saw seven golden lampstands, and in the midst of the lampstands One like the Son of Man" (vv. 12-13). I would like to ask a difficult question: Are the seven golden lampstands in heaven or on earth? Bible scholars throughout the ages are divided into two groups. One group holds the view that the lampstands are in heaven, and the other that they are on earth. Each group has its own reasons and logic. Nevertheless, the seven golden lampstands are neither in heaven nor on earth; they are wherever the church is. Concerning the church, there is no difference between heaven and earth. Before we were saved, heaven and earth were different. Since we have been saved, neither heaven nor earth matter. This may sound peculiar, yet it is the fact. With those who live in the church in reality, there is no difference between heaven and earth.

Wherever the church is, there the dwelling place of God is. Furthermore, wherever the church is, there the lampstand and tabernacle are. The church as the tabernacle and the lampstand is not a matter of location. Therefore, when we read Revelation 1, we should not waste much thought to study whether the seven golden lampstands are on earth or in heaven. These seven golden lampstands are the churches. Where the church is, there is the Lord Jesus, the dwelling place of God, the lampstand, and the Holy Place. The church is not in heaven or on earth, yet the church is also in heaven and on earth. The church can be everywhere. It is a matter not of heaven or earth but of the church. We all love the newly built meeting hall on Jen-Ai Road, but that is not the church. We are the church. If we are not in the meeting hall on Jen-Ai Road, there is no light or lampstand there. There is only a building with reinforced concrete but no tabernacle. When we are here, the tabernacle, the lampstand, and the dwelling place of God are here. If we could be in midair, then the lampstand and the dwelling place of God would be there also. It is not a matter of heaven or earth but a matter of the church. Where the church is, there the dwelling place of God is.

THE SEVEN LAMPS OF FIRE BEING FOR GOD'S MOVE

Now we would like to consider the shining of the seven lamps. This is a driving burden within me, and I hope that I can stir you up! The seven lamps are the lamps of fire burning before the throne; they are not feeble lights but burning lamps of fire. Most of us would understand this as meaning that the lamps first shine on us, and then they burn us. We may say that the seven lamps of fire illuminate us so that whatever our inward condition is, it cannot be concealed. Whether it is genuine or false, it is completely laid bare. We can pretend in front of our husband, wife, or others, but there is no way for us to pretend before the lamps of fire because we are fully illuminated. To be sure, there is this meaning of the lamps of fire. Perhaps others would say that the burning lamps of fire indicate that we are burning in spirit. Every one of us is burning when we are burning in our spirit. This is correct also. However, according to Revelation 4, the emphasis of the seven burning lamps of fire is neither on shining nor on burning.

Perhaps when some hear this word, they may remind me that when I was among you six or seven years ago, I said that the lamps of fire are for burning and illumining us so that we may be burning. Now it seems that I have come back to throw away what I previously said. We may compare this to the view of a man's head. If we look at it from the back, there are no openings, if we look at it from the front, there are five openings, while if we look at it from the side, there is one opening. All three descriptions are correct. In the same way, every truth has several aspects. A brother once wrote and asked me, "In the *Life-study of Romans* you said that the law, as the complete testimony of God, testifies Him fully. However, you also said that we should put the law aside. Are you not contradicting yourself?" Toward God, the function of the law is as a testimony. Nevertheless, in God's dealing with man, the law was only useful in the Old Testament age. In the New Testament age the law is useless. This is the principle of the law, which has been abolished in the New Testament age. However, the morality of the law has not been abolished; on the contrary, it was raised higher by the Lord Jesus in Matthew 5. Therefore, there are several aspects to the law, and we cannot make the one word *law* cover every aspect. As to its function, the law testifies of God, but as to its principle, the law cannot be applied to us today. Once it is applied, it kills us. Today we are in the principle of faith. On the one hand, the morality of the law has been uplifted; on the other hand, the ceremonies of the law have been abolished. This demonstrates that every truth has its different aspects. Yes, with the seven lamps of fire there are the illuminating and the burning aspects. However, there is another aspect that we should know: The seven burning lamps of fire are for the move of God's administration. God's move is not merely an illuminating or a burning.

After this conference the young brothers and sisters in Taipei may go back and say, "We were exhausted in the last ten days. Now we can have a good sleep." Likewise, the brothers from the other countries in Southeast Asia may say, "Oh, in Taipei we were scolded by Brother Lee! Let's forget about it and get some sleep!" In a slightly better way, other brothers may go back and say, "Thank the Lord! The conference was so good. I was really helped. Before, I had no feeling when I scolded my wife. Now, since Brother Lee said that there is a sevenfold light, I dare not scold her. Starting from today I have to be a good husband, because I cannot withstand the shining." These reactions are not the burning of the seven lamps of fire. What then should the burning of the seven lamps of fire produce? After this conference the young ones should take action to go to the different towns and villages in Taiwan for the establishing of churches, and they should go to the schools in the big cities to gain people.

When I returned to Taiwan ten years ago, I was very clear, saying, "Your eyes have to be open. Do not be too busy outwardly. You should work on the young people, the junior highers, and the high schoolers. You should also work on the children until each week there are at least ten thousand children being taught by us. Those who are six or seven years old now will be high schoolers in ten years. If you are willing to do this, you can definitely succeed." The brothers told me at that time that there were twenty-three thousand names on the list of the church in Taipei, comprising at least eight thousand homes. If each family has one or two children, there should be twelve thousand children. When they asked me concerning a place for the children to meet, I said, "There is no need to go to the meeting hall, and it is not necessary to meet on the Lord's Day. You can meet on Saturdays or in the evenings. You can simply meet in the homes of the brothers and sisters. Out of the eight thousand families, you can choose three to four hundred homes to be the places for the children's meetings, with each home holding thirty children. If you continue in this work, you will see how much you can accomplish!" Starting from 1966 and 1967 I have been talking about this very matter and have been expecting the church to practice it, because we do have the basic strength to work it out. If we had worked from that time until now, 1977, ten thousand children would have become high schoolers of sixteen to seventeen years of age. Immediately, there would be ten thousand "seeds" in different high schools. At that time I also said that we had to work on the junior highers, the high schoolers, and the college students to gain several thousand in each category. In this way, the number of children and young people added together would be at least twenty to thirty thousand. Moreover, children increase endlessly. When these ten thousand get out of high school, another ten thousand will take their place. It is a pity that you did not practice what I said!

We thank the Lord that there are so many young working brothers and sisters in Taipei. However, this is still not enough. The church in Taipei has been in existence for twenty-eight years, and many of you brothers and sisters have received many years of nurturing so that each one of you can do a work. Dear brothers and sisters, I hope that the fiery lamps of God are shining here so that your eyes will be opened. Do you know what age this is? The Lord is right before us. Look at the world situation, the condition in Israel, and the situation in the Middle East. The Lord Jesus is right before us. Now is the time for the fiery lamps to shine on us and to motivate us. When the lamps of fire shine on us, we will all move and rise up to take action. When we broke bread last Lord's Day, we had over ten thousand people. If these ten thousand are all stirred up as a result of the shining of the lamps of fire, immediately the gospel will be preached throughout the island of Taiwan, and this testimony will be brought to the whole of Southeast Asia.

CARING FOR NOTHING BUT
BEING DRIVEN BY THE LAMPS OF FIRE

The burning of the fiery lamps is not only for shining and burning but also for motivating. Lightnings, voices, and thunders come forth out of the throne, and before the throne are seven burning lamps of fire for impelling us. Perhaps some would say that they cannot do it. The more we do not do something, the more we cannot do it. This is a principle in the Bible. To everyone who has, more shall be given, and he shall abound; but from him who does not have, that is, who does not use what he has, even that which he has shall be taken away from him (Matt. 25:28-29). We cannot do it simply because we do not do it. I can do it because I have done it many times. The more I do it, the more I can do it.

Dear brothers and sisters, today in the church the seven lamps of fire are burning not only to shine on us and to burn us but even more to motivate us. If there were a raging fire in front of us, would we not run from it? We would not stand here to appreciate it. Once a fire starts burning, everyone moves. When the seven lamps of fire are burning in the local churches, will all the churches in the different localities start moving? Certainly they will! Today we are not only in the Holy Place; we are before the throne, which is the center of God's administration. The throne is God's move and God's economy. The seven lamps of fire are burning here to impel us.

According to my observation, there are at least five thousand active members in the church in Taipei. If every one hundred of you are responsible for a full-timer, at least fifty people can go full-time. Never mind whether or not you are qualified; the Lord is coming soon, so let us serve with our full time. When I was young, I had a very good job. My monthly income was more than enough to cover the expenses of five households. One day, the Lord came to me. He called me and forced me to leave my job to do His work. I said, "O Lord! On what should I depend for my living?" The Lord said, "I will be responsible." I believed, yet I had unbelief. However, since the Lord wanted me, there was nothing I could do. Therefore, I said to Him, "O Lord, I will follow You. I am determined to eat the roots of trees and drink water from the mountain to preach the gospel for You." Hence, I resigned from my job. When my father-in-law heard this, he shook his head and said, "There is no fool like you. Can't you go to work in the daytime and preach messages at night and on Sundays? Besides, your income can help those who are in need. Now that you have forsaken your job, what is your family going to live on?" I said in my heart, "I will eat tree roots and drink water from the mountain," but I praise the Lord that for these many years, I never had to eat tree roots or drink water from the mountain. Hallelujah, the Lord is living!

When I was sent by the work to Taiwan, the work did not supply even one dollar for me. For a household of twelve, I only had a little over three hundred dollars. However, the land for the meeting halls of several principal churches on this island were purchased with the money from my ministry here. You may ask me, "Brother Lee, where does your money come from?" There is always a place it comes from: It descends from heaven. The Lord knows that I am prepared to eat tree roots and drink water from the mountain. Nevertheless, praise the Lord, He has given us what we have not asked for, even superabundantly above all that we ask or think.

My point is this, brothers and sisters: Our God is a trustworthy God, and He is true and living. Young people, there is no need to consider your future. The most glorious future is to serve Him. No other future is more honorable than this. Do not look at the present. At present, you may ask what you will do without a job. There is no way according to the earth, but there is a way according to heaven. There is no way with man, but there is a way with God. I encourage you to know the age; the time is short. The throne is in the church, and the seven lamps before the throne are burning here, not only to illuminate and burn us but even more to motivate us, to impel us. How happy I am to see many young ones rising up to be the succeeding generations! I do not want to merely excite you, but I hope that among us the seven lamps of fire are burning. The Lord is here and He is speaking. Do not be worried about your future and your environment; the environment is in His hand. We thank the Lord that He has blessed Taiwan, and we believe that He will continue to bless it. We should seize the

opportunity and try our best to preach the gospel and bring
the testimony of the church to different cities, towns, and villages; this is our responsibility. Today the seven lamps of fire
are burning before the throne in the Holy Place.

CHAPTER FIVE

THE SEVEN EYES OF GOD
FOR TRANSFUSION

Scripture Reading: Zech. 4:10; 2 Chron. 16:9a; Rev. 5:6; 4:5; Psa. 33:18; 32:8

THE SEVEN LAMPS
ENLIGHTENING AND BURNING

We have seen that the golden lampstand involves a number of items. In the previous chapter we saw that the seven lamps of the golden lampstand ultimately become the seven lamps of fire. Do not think that the seven shining lamps and the seven lamps of fire are completely identical. They are very similar but they are not absolutely identical. The seven lamps in Exodus were seven shining lamps without any burning fire. Lamps are usually shining but not burning; however, when we come to Revelation, the seven lamps on the lampstands are not only brightly shining but also burning. Revelation 4 says that lightnings, voices, and thunders come forth out of the throne and that there are seven lamps of fire burning before the throne. By looking at this picture, we can see that God wants to have His move, His government, and His economy and that God's move is in the lamps of fire. There are seven lamps of fire burning before the throne of God, that is, before God Himself. Not only is there light for shining and enlightening, but there is also fire for burning. Furthermore, this burning is for motivating. In a remarkable way Revelation 4 also says that these seven burning lamps of fire are the seven Spirits of God, and chapter 5 says that the seven Spirits are the seven eyes of God.

The Seed and the Harvest
of the Revelation in the Bible
concerning the Golden Lampstand

We should never consider that these matters are in the Bible in a random, coincidental way. The revelation in the Bible is progressive. It may be compared to a seed planted in the soil. At first, all we know is that a seed has been planted and is buried there, but we cannot see anything. After a period of time we can see a sprout coming forth, but it is so small that it is difficult to distinguish what the plant is. After another period of time the stem comes out, and gradually small branches appear with leaves on them. Sometime afterward, it blossoms and bears fruit, and last, there is a harvest. At that time everyone is clear at one glance what kind of plant it is.

Most of the biblical revelations are sown as seeds in Genesis, but a small number are sown in the second book, Exodus. The seed of the golden lampstand is sown not in Genesis but in Exodus, and the growth is in 1 Kings. The golden lampstand in 1 Kings is in the holy temple; yet, although the growth of the seed is there, the golden lampstand is still vague because we cannot see its relationship to the Spirit. When we finally come to Zechariah 4, we see that the emphasis of the golden lampstand is not Christ but the Spirit, who is signified by the olive oil within the lamps. Therefore, in Zechariah there is a further development. This is a big step, but there is still no harvest. Where is the harvest? It is in Revelation. In Revelation we see that the golden lampstand has developed and arrived at its ultimate goal—the church. With the church there is Christ, and with the church there is also the Spirit. The church is the reproduction, the reprint, of the Spirit with Christ. In this reprint we see the Spirit, and we also see Christ. These two— Christ and the Spirit—added together become the church. What is the church? Today we can strongly say that the church is the manifestation of Christ added together with the Spirit. When Christ and the Spirit are manifested together, that is the church, and that is also the golden lampstand. I hope that all the saints in the Lord's recovery can have their eyes opened to know the church to this extent.

The Golden Lampstand in Exodus—
the Shining Lamps for Enlightening

There are seven lamps on the golden lampstand. In Exodus the seven lamps enlightened the darkness so that the priests who served God could move in the realm of God's presence, that is, in the Holy Place. There was no door or window in the Holy Place, so without the golden lampstand there would be no light, and the priest could not know what to do or how to move when he entered to serve God. In the Holy Place there was a golden lampstand, upon which were seven lamps shining forth brightly. A priest who entered into the Holy Place immediately knew God's move and God's economy.

The Golden Lampstand in Revelation—
the Lamps of Fire for Burning

In Revelation the seven shining lamps have developed into seven burning lamps of fire. They are not only shining lamps but also fiery lamps—burning lamps of fire, lamps burning with fire. The lamps of fire imply judgment. The seven lamps are not only enlightening and burning; they are also judging. Actually, the seven shining lamps in Revelation 4 become seven great furnaces burning before the throne of God.

We must remember 1 Corinthians 3:10-13: "Let each man take heed how he builds upon it...But if anyone builds upon the foundation gold, silver, precious stones, wood, grass, stubble, the work of each will become manifest." How will it become manifest? One day each man's work will be "revealed by fire" (v. 13). If our work in the church is gold, silver, and precious stones, that is excellent, for it can stand the test of fire. However, if our work is wood, grass, and stubble, it is fuel to be consumed by the fire. Therefore, with the seven lamps there are not only the enlightening and the burning, but also there is judgment in the burning. We must know that whenever God moves, He judges. A dragging, hesitant person cannot follow God's move. When God moves, He always moves with His judgment.

We all like bright lamps. In our house at night, when all around us is darkness, we certainly like to have a shining lamp for illumination, but no one wants to have a lamp of fire. If we returned home and discovered that our house was on fire, not by the enlightening of shining lamps but by the burning of lamps of fire, we would be greatly alarmed. Do not forget that the golden lampstand in Exodus has the shining lamps, whereas in Revelation it has the burning lamps. In Exodus, the emphasis of the golden lampstand is on its shining; there is no implication of burning. In Revelation, however, the golden lampstand not only shines, but it has advanced from shining to become burning lamps of fire.

Experiencing the Burning
of the Seven Lamps

We all like to testify that we saw the light when we came into the church, but what did the light do shortly afterward? Eventually, we were burned by the light that we saw. Initially the light that we saw was a shining, but ultimately it was a burning. The old concepts, the old thoughts, the poison of tradition, and other matters were all burned away. We may compare these to bags of grass. In the past we carried many "grass bags," and we treasured them so much that we were reluctant to discard them even after we came into the church. Many brothers and sisters came from Christianity; this is especially true in the West. When certain ones came to their first meeting, I secretly observed in my heart that they had come with "bundles of grass bags." Nevertheless, when they came back to the meeting a week later, I could see that the "top bundle" was in flames. They were not aware of it, but I saw it. I was happy inwardly, and I thanked and praised the Lord, saying, "Let it burn!" Another two weeks would go by, and I could see that all the "grass bags" were burned to nothing, and the fire had spread to the rest of their being. In the past some among us were pastors or traveling preachers. They did a great deal of "grass" work and were full of "grass." However, when they came into the church, they saw the light, and after a short time, the light became a burning fire. What burned them? It was not doctrines but light. The light of the Holy Place in the church eventually becomes the fire burning before the throne.

Is this not your experience? I trust that the sisters have had this kind of experience. When some first came into the church, they saw the light, but within a few days this light began to burn, and it burned one thing after another. At the beginning, they may have said, "It is so good to be in the church! It is so sweet to have the Lord's presence! Thank and praise the Lord!" However, before they could finish saying, "Thank and praise the Lord," something within them began to trouble them, saying, "What about changing your attitude toward your husband?" They may have said, "O Lord, I am not the only one at fault; he is also wrong. Why should I change but not him? Since he is the head, he should change first. If he will deal with his sins by confessing his mistakes to me, I will do the same for him. I will not confess my mistakes before he does." Nevertheless, the burning within those sisters did not allow them to eat or sleep well. Previously, it was, "O Lord, the church life is so sweet!" but now it is not so sweet. Rather, it is like bitter medicine because there is nothing they can do except confess. What causes this? It is the burning.

Some say, "Why are you the church, and we are not?" Everyone fights to be the church. Let them go ahead and fight, but if they want to be the church, they have to take the bitter medicine and experience the burning. Let the "grass bags" and their temper be burned away. When everything is completely burned away, there is the golden lampstand. The golden lampstand comes out of burning. In a recent combined meeting for the breaking of bread, the brothers and sisters were excited when they saw the large bread spread on the table. However, when the time came for the bread to be broken, the shining light may have become the burning fire, and the Lord may have said to some, "Do you want to break this bread? Have you dealt with the differences of opinion you have with the brothers and sisters?" This is the burning of the seven lamps, and it is our experience.

Knowing the Mystery of the Golden Lampstand by the Lord's Mercy

Spiritual things cannot be thoroughly explained even with a thousand words. In these chapters we have seen the golden lampstand. The golden lampstand is Jehovah, Jehovah is the Lamb, the Lamb is the stone, and the stone is God. I believe that we all now know these new terms. Nevertheless, if we speak them to people, they will think that we are crazy because they do not understand what we are talking about. To be sure, even some of the professors of the Bible in the seminaries do not understand this. Even though they have the Bible in their hands, they do not know these things. However, today we know them by the Lord's mercy. We know that the golden lampstand is Jehovah, and Jehovah, the God who has a relationship with us, is our Lamb. We also know that this Lamb is the stone that was engraved by God, and that in one day this engraving removed all the iniquity of God's people. This stone, eventually, is just God. These things could not be more clear even if we listened to ten thousand more words. What is the church? The church is the golden lampstand, the golden lampstand is Jehovah, Jehovah is the Lamb, the Lamb is the stone, and the stone is God.

We cannot use human words to explain the church. It is too mysterious, but we can state it in this way: The church is the reproduction of the Spirit with Christ. Today if we ask those in the seminary what it means that the church is the reproduction of the Spirit with Christ, they may say, "We do not have such a thing in our systematic theology. We only have the church. We do not say that the church is the reproduction of the Spirit with Christ. We don't understand this." However, we all can understand. Even the youngest among us can understand. What is the church? The church is the reproduction, the manifestation, of the Spirit with Christ.

God's Move with Judgment

The golden lampstand is first a matter of the enlightening of the seven lamps and then of the burning of the lamps of fire. The burning is for the move, and with the move is the judgment. Whenever God moves, He judges. God never does a dragging, hesitant work. He never carries any "grass bags"; He is always clear-cut. Whatever is according to His will, He receives; whatever is not, He rejects. Judges 7 tells us that when God wanted Gideon to smite the Midianites, Gideon had

over thirty thousand men with him. God came into this situation in order to move, and His moving was His judging. God
told Gideon, "The people are still too many. Bring them down
to the water, and I will test them for you there" (v. 4). The test
of drinking the water was a judgment. When they drank the
water, they were tested. Only three hundred could follow
Gideon in his action, and the rest had to return home. God's
move is His burning, and His burning is the judgment for His
move.

THE SEVEN EYES OF GOD
FOR TRANSFUSING

After the seven lamps of fire burn in us, they become seven
eyes. It is wonderful that the shining lamps become the lamps
of fire, and the lamps of fire become the eyes. We all know that
the eyes are the most lovely part of a person. If a person closes
his eyes, we cannot see what is lovely in him. A person's love-
liness is in his eyes. Thank the Lord that the shining and
burning lamps eventually become the lovely eyes. I can testify
that anyone who has gone through God's burning, judging,
and purifying, and whose "grass bags" have been burned away
by God, can say, "O God! I thank You that the burning lamps of
fire are the lovely eyes." These seven lamps are the seven eyes
of God.

Perhaps some may say that the seven eyes are fearful, because angry eyes are frightening. The seven lamps are the
seven Spirits of God, the seven eyes of God. Are these seven
eyes fearful or lovely? One may say that they are sometimes
fearful and sometimes lovely, but whether the eyes are fearful
or lovely depends not on Him but on us. If we behave as the
proper children of God, His eyes are lovely, but if we are
naughty, His eyes are fearful. Nevertheless, whether they are
fearful or lovely, at least they are not just lamps of fire. We
thank and praise Him that they are still His eyes. I can testify,
and I believe that many can also testify, that these seven are
the seven eyes to us and not only the seven lamps of fire.

Eyes are not only for seeing but also for transfusing. What
does transfusing mean? It is to transmit a person's inner
being into the one he is looking at. When a brother whom I

delight in comes to me and I look at him, the joy and sweet-ness within me is transfused into him through my eyes. However, if I see a brother who is very naughty and say within my heart, "Oh! It's him," these thoughts within me are like-wise transfused into him. To transfuse is to infuse. Whether the transfusion is of love or of fear, God has been transfused into us.

The Church Being the Place for God's Transfusion

Here I would like to use a new phrase: *The church is the place where God transfuses.* Have you ever heard such a phrase? Every time we meet together, we allow God to transfuse Him-self into us. This is the reality of the church. Previously, many of us were in Christianity, in the old denominations. We dressed up properly to "go to church" every Sunday morning, and near the end of the service, the offering plate would be passed, and we would put money in it. Can we say from our conscience that God's transfusing was there? I do not know what was transmitted there, but it was definitely not the place where God was transfusing. However, when we come to the church meetings, we feel that we are sitting before the Lord and that His eyes are looking at us. If we obey Him, we feel that He is lovely. If we disobey Him, He is still lovely, but we are a little ashamed. We may say, "O Lord, in the past week I disobeyed You. Lord, forgive me and wash me with Your pre-cious blood." We all have had such an experience. This is the transfusion and infusion of the Lord's inner being into us for our transformation. Transformation is not a change caused by a shining light; rather, it is the transfusing of the Lord's lov-able person into us. After such an experience we may return home with tears, saying, "O Lord! Have mercy on me this week. I don't want to sin against You again. I want to please You." However, we still do not know Him enough. Our heart is right, but we are wrong because we do not know that we cannot please the Lord. We are like a centipede that can only crawl on the ground but wants to fly in the air. It is as if we are saying, "O Lord, I was crawling on the ground last week; not once did I fly in the air to please You. I really sinned against You. Starting from this week I don't want to crawl on the ground. I want to fly in the air with You." However, after such a prayer at the beginning of the week, we may start "crawling on the ground" the same night and continue for the whole week. Then on the following Lord's Day when we come to the meeting, the seven eyes of God may say, "Here you are again!" and we may repeat our prayer of confession. However, the Lord may say, "Do not cry! I do not blame you at all. You are a 'centipede,' so I have no intention that you would fly. Do you not know that I am the flying life?" Sometimes, however, the Lord does not say anything; He just transfuses. This transfusion goes on week by week until the "centipede" begins to "fly." This will amaze our family; they will not know what has happened. They will not be able to describe it, but they will sense that there is something wonderful in us and that we have had a great change. Such an experience is the reality of the church.

The seven eyes are in the church. We must not forget that the seven eyes are on the lampstand, and the lampstand is in the Holy Place. If we are not in the Holy Place, we do not have the lampstand, and without the lampstand we cannot have the seven eyes. The Holy Place is the church, and the lampstand is also the church. To receive the transfusion of the seven eyes we must be in the church. To be in the church is not merely a matter of listening to messages or giving messages. These are small matters. Some elderly sisters can testify that many times after coming to the meetings, they cannot remember anything that was said. However, they do remember that when they go to the meetings, something touches them and enters into them, although they cannot explain it clearly. They feel that it is so good to go to the meetings, and it is a loss not to go. That is why after going to a meeting on the Lord's Day, they still go on the following Tuesday, and they make it a rule to go again on Thursday. Although they cannot remember clearly what is said, they feel so good within. This is the characteristic of the churches in the Lord's recovery.

There are some who say that the church has a way of capturing people. After coming to meet with us and listening to two messages, they say, people are "glued," and they go to the meeting hall every day. The old ones go, and the young ones also go; the men go, and the women also go; they go on the Lord's Day and also on Tuesday; they go in the morning and also in the evening. Someone once asked me what our secret is. The secret is the seven lamps of fire and the seven eyes. Whether or not we are the church does not depend on outward organization; it depends on whether there are the seven eyes among us. These seven eyes are not only for shining on us but also for transfusing God Himself into us. Even if one is a highly educated and intelligent university professor, this does not mean that he has the proper understanding. In 1947 there was a revival in the church in Shanghai, where there was a university professor who loved me very much. He said, "Brother Lee, I would feel good just to accompany you and help you carry your Bible bag." Nevertheless, the problem was that even though he was a professor in a medical school and had listened to all my messages, he understood nearly nothing at all. In contrast, I have seen some sisters in Shanghai who were quite elderly. They could not speak Mandarin properly or read the Bible smoothly, but when they listened to my messages, they understood every single one. This is the characteristic of the church. The church is not those with degrees or those with big minds. The church is a group of people who have experienced God's transfusion. God is able to transfuse Himself into them. I can truly testify for those elderly sisters in Shanghai that they were clear within. God could transfuse His being into them.

The effectiveness of our work lies here. If we use our mind to speak mere knowledge, although we can make a professor understand us, there is no transfusion of God. The secret of our work does not lie in how many good messages we have given. Rather, it hinges on how much God has been transfused into others after each meeting or message. This is what makes a difference. Some people are very eloquent, and when they give a sermon, it is like music, but in the end there is no transfusion of God. We thank and praise Him that the seven lamps are the seven eyes. Today the Lamb has seven eyes, not seven lamps; likewise, the stone has seven eyes, not seven lamps. The eyes are here gazing at us to transfuse God into us.

God Guiding Us with His Eyes

Second Chronicles 16:9 says, "The eyes of Jehovah run to and fro throughout all the earth." Today God's eyes are running to and fro, seeking those whose heart is perfect towards Him. Psalm 32:8 says, "I will instruct you and teach you concerning the way you should go; / I will counsel you; my eye is upon you." The Lord guides us not mainly with words or other indications but with His eyes. The guiding of the eyes is the most intimate kind, and it is used between those who are intimate. When two very intimate people speak with one another, they may not necessarily use their mouth; instead, they may use their eyes. Very often when I visit the homes of brothers and sisters, I notice that the couples do not always converse with their mouth. Just with one glance, the other partner will know if it is time to brew the tea or take care of other matters. Sometimes I also understand what the glance means; when I look at their eyes, I know, for example, that it is time for me to leave. When the husband and wife have been close to each other for a long time, perhaps for thirty or forty years, the husband has become the wife, and the wife has become the husband. This is because they have been mutually transfusing themselves into one another for thirty years. Only this makes a sweet couple.

In the same way, after we have been in the church for a long period of time, what God is, what the Lord is, is gradually infused into us. This is not something we can pick up intentionally; it is a result of a long period of time. He has been transfusing Himself into us all the time. We have at least four to five meetings a week, and in each meeting there are two hours of transfusion. We can compare this to charging a battery. When a battery is fully charged, it can run for two days, but when its electricity is almost used up, it has to be brought back for recharging. Then after being recharged, it runs again. I have been "charged" for forty-five years. This is the transfusion of the seven eyes.

The church is something that is too mysterious, beyond human description. Many brothers and sisters may be able to testify that before attending this conference, their understanding of the church was not thorough, but after hearing these messages they clearly see what the church is. The church is the golden lampstand, and the seven lamps on the golden lampstand are the lamps of fire, which after burning us become the eyes. The eyes are transfusing and sometimes rebuking. If we enter into a meeting and do not have the sense of transfusion, we have to question whether it is really the church. Perhaps it is the church, but it is not proper; it has problems because it does not give light or transfuse God. It is as if the electric fuse has burned out, and the supply of electricity has been cut off. When this is the case, the "fuse" should be quickly changed. Certain elders or young brothers know how to do this by releasing some prayers. Then the "electricity" is reconnected, and the whole meeting once again has the transfusion. This is the nature of the church. Without the transfusion of God, we do not have the church.

THE SEVEN SPIRITS SUPPLYING LIFE

The seven eyes that carry out the transfusion are the seven Spirits. The seven lamps are the seven Spirits, the seven eyes are also the seven Spirits, and the seven Spirits are the Holy Spirit. When I was young, after I had been saved for a few years, whenever the Holy Spirit was mentioned, I felt puzzled. I dared not say that there was no Holy Spirit, but I did not know what and where the Holy Spirit was. Gradually, I came to know that the Holy Spirit is the transfusion of God, and I know it more so today. After attending meetings for a long time, we may become accustomed to them. When it is time to go to a meeting, we simply pick up our Bible bag and go. However, after sitting down for two minutes, a certain power or condition that is unexplainable begins to touch us from within. Originally, we did not have a proper heart and were indifferent, but just by sitting in the meeting, we are touched within. Perhaps in the meeting no one speaks either of the Holy Spirit or of the transfusion of God, but we are touched simply by sitting there. Sometimes we are so thankful for this, and sometimes we are full of self-reproach. Sometimes we are enlightened, and sometimes we are rebuked. Sometimes we are released, and sometimes we have peace and are watered. What is this? It is the move and work of the Spirit; that is, it is the Spirit Himself.

The more a meeting is full of the nature of the church, the more it is full of the operation of the Spirit, which is the seven Spirits transfusing and infusing. The Spirit is life, and the seven Spirits are for us to receive the supply of life and to be equipped in life. The lamps have become the fire, the fire has become the eyes, and the eyes are the Spirit. God first shines within us, then He burns in us, and then He transfuses and infuses Himself into us. The issue is that we have the supply of life and are equipped with life. Eventually, our function is manifested in the church, and we grow in life and are built up together with others. As a result, we are not merely the church but the functioning church in which all the saints minister. We are not only enlightened, burned, and infused, but we also receive the supply of life and are equipped in life. Thus we become the functioning members in the Body.

When we turn to the Spirit, everything is life. The lamps are for illuminating, the fire is for burning, the eyes are for transfusing, and the Spirit is altogether for the supply of life and the equipping in life. This is the church. First, there are the golden lampstand, Jehovah, the Lamb, the stone, and God. Then there are the lamps, the fire, the eyes, and the Spirit. Only when we have thoroughly understood these nine items do we know what the church is. The church is a matter of these nine items. When we come into the church, we are first enlightened by the shining lamps. Then there is the burning of the lamps of fire. Then the eyes observe and care for us, transfusing what God is and what the Lord is into us. Last, there is the Spirit who is life with the supply of life and the equipping of life. All this in totality is the church.

CHAPTER SIX

THE BURNING LAMPS OF FIRE
BECOMING THE FLOWING RIVERS

Scripture Reading: Exo. 17:5-6; 1 Cor. 10:1-4; John 7:37-39; 1 Cor. 12:13; Rev. 1:4; 4:5; 5:6; 22:1, 17; 2:1, 7a; 21:23

JOHN'S WRITINGS AND THE BOOK OF EXODUS MUTUALLY REFLECTING EACH OTHER

The Bible is a wonderful book. In Exodus when the children of Israel were thirsty in their wandering in the wilderness, God told Moses to take his staff and strike the rock. When he struck the rock, water flowed out of it, the people drank, and their thirst was quenched. We cannot find such a story in any other classical book. Although this story seems to be simple, its connotation is not simple. In Exodus we cannot find the significance of this story, but when we come to the New Testament, we find John 7:37-38, which says, "Now on the last day, the great day of the feast, Jesus stood and cried out, saying, If anyone thirsts, let him come to Me and drink. He who believes into Me, as the Scripture said, out of his innermost being shall flow rivers of living water."

The main points in the writings of John are the same as those in Exodus. In Exodus there is the lamb, and John writes, "Behold, the Lamb of God" (1:29). At the end of Exodus there is the tabernacle, and at the conclusion of his writings, John also says, "Behold, the tabernacle of God is with men" (Rev. 21:3). In Exodus there is the lampstand, a crucial item in the tabernacle related to the administration of God and the actions of those who serve God, and in John's writings, the churches are called the lampstands. By this we can see that the writings of John and Exodus reflect each other.

As we have seen, John refers to the living water that flowed out of the rock in Exodus. John speaks about this in a marvelous way, saying that if anyone thirsts, he may come to the Lord Jesus and drink. He does not say that the Lord Jesus is the rock; rather, he says that out of the innermost being of the one who believes into the Lord shall flow rivers of living water. According to the Greek, *rivers* is plural. It is not one river but many rivers. The connotation here is that the drinkers eventually become small "rocks." In Exodus the water flowed out of a single rock to quench the people's thirst; in John's writings, the living water flows out, but the flowing is not out of one rock but out of many "small rocks." When we drink the water supplied by the Lord Jesus, we become "small rocks," each one flowing out rivers of living water, river after river. We do not flow out only one river; we flow out many rivers from within us.

Exodus is the "nursery" of a great number of truths, and John's writings are the "farm" of the truths. In Exodus there is one rock, whereas in John's Gospel there are many small rocks. In Exodus there is one river, but in John's Gospel there are many rivers. Not only the rocks are many, but even the rivers that flow out of each rock are many. This signifies multiplication and increase. One rock has become many rocks, and one river has become many rivers. Perhaps some may argue that this is merely our own interpretation. However, if we read 1 Corinthians 10, we will see Paul's interpretation. Paul says, "All our fathers were under the cloud, and all passed through the sea; and all were baptized unto Moses in the cloud and in the sea; and all ate the same spiritual food, and all drank the same spiritual drink" (vv. 1-4a). How wonderful this is! In Exodus the water flowed out of the rock on Mount Horeb, yet Paul says that it was spiritual drink. Was that physical drink or spiritual drink? We all should say, "According to figure, it was physical, but according to reality, it was spiritual." In Exodus the water that flowed out of the rock was a figure, a sign, a symbol, a picture, portraying a spiritual condition. Exodus uses physical water to signify spiritual water, which is the Spirit.

This water is not merely the Holy Spirit. Before the Lord

was smitten, before He as the smitten rock was cleft, the Holy Spirit was already there, but "the Spirit" was not yet. We may say that before the rock was smitten, there was already rain water in the atmosphere, but it was not until the rock was smitten and cleft that the rain water became the living water flowing out of the rock. Before the rock was smitten, the rain water was there, but the living water was not yet. This signifies that before the Lord Jesus was crucified and resurrected, the Holy Spirit was there, but "the Spirit" was not yet. When the Lord Jesus was cleft by being smitten on the cross, immediately there came out blood and water (John 19:34). That was the flowing out of the living water, of which John tells us that Jesus spoke "concerning the Spirit, whom those who believed into Him were about to receive" (7:39). John points out clearly that the water which flowed out of the smitten Jesus is the Spirit.

In 1 Corinthians 10:4 Paul tells us that what the children of Israel drank was spiritual drink. What Paul says next is even more marvelous. He says that this water came out of a spiritual rock which followed them. Paul says that the rock was following the children of Israel. How can we explain this? Could that rock walk? Was it drawn by a wagon? If we ask orthodox theologians today, they may say that Paul is twisting God's word. Perhaps they would ask Paul, "The rock smitten by Moses was on the mountain, and it remained there after it had been smitten. How can you say that the rock was following them?" The rock is in the same principle as the water that the Israelites drank. As we have said previously, the water was physical, yet as a symbol or picture it denotes the spiritual water. A picture of a tiger does not move, but in reality, the tiger itself moves. In the same way, the rock in the picture does not move, but in God's eyes, that rock is Christ. "They drank of a spiritual rock which followed them, and the rock was Christ" (v. 4b). As a physical object, the rock could not move, but as Christ, the rock moved and followed the Israelites. Wherever the Israelites went, the rock followed them there. Hallelujah, we are confident that in our midst there is a rock, which is a spiritual rock! When we meet on Jen-Ai Road, this rock is here with us; when we meet in a stadium, this rock is there; when we go to Mount Ali, this rock also goes to the mountaintop. This is a spiritual rock that follows us. The rock is Christ, and the water, according to our study of the Bible, is the Spirit. The water flowing out of the rock refers to the Spirit flowing out of Christ. Here we have another problem: Orthodox theology teaches that the Holy Spirit is the Holy Spirit, that Christ is Christ, and that the two are completely separate. But are these two absolutely separate? As we have seen, the Lamb is Christ and the seven eyes of the Lamb are the Spirit. To say that They are absolutely separate, since the Holy Spirit is one and Christ is another, is to remove the eyes from the body, saying, "The eyes are the eyes, and the person is the person." In principle, this is the doctrine of the Trinity as taught by orthodox traditional theology.

ORTHODOX TRADITIONAL THEOLOGY BEING UNRELIABLE

I would like to take this opportunity to show, especially to the young brothers and sisters, that the "orthodox" doctrine concerning the Trinity is unreliable. Orthodox traditional theologians believe in the Nicene Creed, which was established in the council held in Nicaea in A.D. 325. Prior to that time, in the second and third centuries, the debates among the early Bible scholars, the so-called church fathers, reached a peak. The debates were mostly concerning the Triune God, the relationship among the three of the Triune God, and the Person of Christ—who Christ is and whether He is God or man. For two hundred years they argued to such an extent that they were at a stalemate. It was at this juncture, around A.D. 310, that Constantine the Great obtained the Roman Empire and became emperor. He accepted Christianity as the state religion of Rome and encouraged the Roman people to be baptized and join the church. Anyone who was baptized to join the church was given a set of garments and a certain amount of silver. Hence, at that time thousands of the people of Rome joined the church. Formerly the Roman Empire persecuted Christianity, but beginning from Constantine the Great, it changed its tactic and began to welcome Christianity, which then became the most powerful entity in the Roman Empire.

At that time, Constantine the Great tried to discourage the Bible scholars from constant quarreling with each other so that he could maintain a proper order within the empire. Thus, in A.D. 325 he issued a decree to gather all the Bible scholars, including the bishops in different places, to Nicaea for a council. The chairman of that council was Constantine himself, and the bishops, the Bible scholars, debated in front of him. At the conclusion of the debates, a creed was decided upon, which is called the Nicene Creed. To this day, it is commonly believed and recognized by the Roman Catholic Church and the ortho- dox Protestant churches, such as the Episcopalian Church, the Methodist Church, and other large denominations.

The Nicene Creed speaks of the Triune God, referring to the Holy Father, the Holy Son, and the Holy Spirit, but not one word is said about the Holy Spirit being the life-giving Spirit. It was not until A.D. 381 that a further word was added con- cerning the life-giving Spirit. Despite the addition of this further word, regardless of how we study the creeds, we still cannot find the seven Spirits. Today in the New Testament there are the Holy Spirit, "the Spirit," the life-giving Spirit, and the seven Spirits, but in the Nicene Creed there are no seven Spirits.

While fighting the battle for the truth in America, we have said to some, "You say that your basis is the creeds, but we say that the creeds are incomplete. Our basis is not the creeds but the Bible." The Lord raised up His recovery in China more than fifty years ago. Thank the Lord, at that time we became clear that we should not take any creed as our basis, because the creeds are incomplete. We must come back to the Bible, which is complete. We asked certain ones, "Do you have the seven Spirits in your creed?" The answer of course was no. For this reason I quoted to them a Chinese saying: "You have cut the feet to fit the shoes." The Nicene Creed may be likened to a small pair of shoes made in A.D. 325. At that time, the church's knowledge of the Bible was like a small pair of feet. Hence, it was quite comfortable to put the shoes on the feet. However, the church's knowledge of the Bible is always improving. The earth cannot be improved, but mankind's knowledge of the earth is improving. Before Columbus's time, people thought that the earth was flat or square; they did not know that the earth is round. The globe does not progress, but man's discovery concerning the globe is progressing. The same is true with the Bible. The Bible cannot be improved; it has been completed once for all. However, our knowledge of the biblical truths is improving by our discoveries.

In A.D. 325 those Bible scholars, those bishops, who came together, knew the Bible, but the measure of their knowledge was small. Therefore, they made a "size-five shoe" for people to wear. At that time the ordinary people's knowledge of the Bible was at most "size five," so they were able to wear that small pair of shoes. But from A.D. 325 to the present time, through the course of more than sixteen hundred years, Christians' knowledge of the Bible has progressed with more discoveries and more light, not only from Matthew to Acts, but from Acts to the Epistles, and in particular today through the Epistles to Revelation. In Revelation we have seen the seven Spirits. Today the "feet" of Christians' knowledge of the Bible are "size eight," yet they try to put them into "size-five shoes." Therefore, I said to the American theologians, "What you are doing is cutting our feet to make them fit into your small shoes."

This challenge has gone out, but up to this day I have not yet heard their answer. They cannot answer. They say that we should take the creeds as our basis, but the creeds do not say anything about the seven Spirits. What then shall we do? Should we cut off the seven Spirits? Do we follow the Bible or the creeds? The seven Spirits are not in the creeds but in the Bible. Do we care for the seven Spirits? We do. Do we, then, care for the creeds? We do not. Thank the Lord, none of us cares for the creeds. As early as the winter of 1925 I cast away the creeds. We thank and praise the Lord that we have not only Matthew, John, Acts, Romans, 1 and 2 Corinthians, and the other Epistles, but also Revelation.

Many say that the three of the Trinity are three individual persons—the Holy Spirit is the Holy Spirit, the Son is the Son, and the Father is the Father. Recently, a number of us went to the Holy Land to see Jerusalem, but before that we also went to see Rome and the Vatican. In the Vatican there is a cathedral, inside which, on the walls of every room, are the best ancient oil paintings. One of the paintings is a portrait of the Triune God: an old father sitting down with a long beard, a middle-aged son standing, and a dove flying above. Another picture had an additional figure, Mary, standing in the middle. This is the Trinity in the teaching of the Vatican. The Father is that white-bearded old father, the Son is that middle-aged son, and the Holy Spirit is the dove flying above. They have only a partial scriptural basis for this concept. What they have is seemingly true, but in reality it is false; it is superficial knowledge.

Apparently, this is the doctrine of the Trinity taught by traditional theologians. We would ask them, "Is the rock Christ? Is the living water the Spirit?" If the answer to both questions is yes, then are Christ and the Spirit divided and separated? They are not, because the living water flows out of Christ. Furthermore, the Lamb is Christ, and the eyes of the Lamb are the Spirit. Since the eyes are a part of the body, the seven eyes of the Lamb are a part of the Lamb; the two cannot be divided. The picture of the rock and the water, which is clearer than any number of words can make it, indicates that the Holy Spirit is the flowing out of Christ. When Christ is infused into us, He is the Spirit. How can one person be infused into another person? It is through the eyes. When a person infuses himself through his eyes, he infuses the reality of what he is. In the same way, the Spirit as the reality of Christ is infused into the saints. Hence, there is no way to separate the Spirit from Christ. To separate Christ from the Spirit is like separating the living water from the rock. Once we separate the living water from the rock, the living water is without a source, and the rock is without a flow. The living water is the flow of the rock, and the rock is the source of the living water. The two are two yet one; they are indivisible, just as the eyes and the body are inseparable.

THE BURNING LAMPS OF FIRE
BECOMING THE FLOWING RIVERS OF WATER

Exodus refers to the flowing of the living water, and John's writings also speak of the flowing of the living water, but there is a difference. There is something more in John's writings than in Exodus. In Exodus we cannot see the seven burning lamps of fire, but in the record in Revelation there are seven lamps of fire burning before the throne. Actually, they are a great fire burning to execute God's judgment and carry out God's work. This is the burning of the seven lamps of fire before the throne, which are the seven Spirits. However, at the end of Revelation, these seven lamps of fire become a river of water of life. At the beginning of Revelation are the seven burning lamps of fire, but at the end of Revelation the lamps of fire are no more; instead, there is a flowing river of water.

When we first came into the church, we sensed that there was light here, and we sensed the shining of the light. However, after being in the church for a period of time, we sense that the shining light becomes a burning fire. If we continue to remain in the church and allow this light to shine on us and this fire to burn us, after such constant shining and burning, the fire turns into the water of life flowing in us. It is possible that within one morning watch we may experience all three aspects. When we first begin our morning watch, we may sense that the light is very bright, as a bright lamp shining. Then after ten minutes we may have a strong feeling that the bright lamp has become a great fire. First there is the shining, and then there is burning. During the remainder of the morning watch, we may be burned continually, perhaps for forty minutes. All our sins are searched out and burned completely. After the burning, we may sense that the smoke, the flames, and the glow of the fire are gone. All that is left is the shining light of the lamp, and immediately we have the feeling that the flame has become the water of life flowing within us. Then during the last ten minutes of that morning watch, the water of life flows, and we are drinking of it.

I believe we all have had this kind of experience. Sometimes within half an hour we can have all three experiences: first the shining, then the burning, and eventually the flowing of the living water of life. The shining exposes our true condition. When we were without the shining, we felt that we were not bad and that no one was as perfect as we were, but after we came into the church and entered into the light, right away our true condition was completely exposed. During times of shining, we discover that we are not all right, we feel that we are not as good as others, and we feel that we are too pitiful. After five minutes of this kind of shining by the light, the shining becomes a burning. Hence, we abhor ourselves; sometimes we beat our breast and hate ourselves, thinking that we are the most wicked persons on earth. Five minutes before, we were the best persons on earth; now we are the worst ones. We confess and weep, and the fire continues to burn for twenty more minutes until there is nothing more to burn. At this time the burning fire becomes the flowing water. The living water flows within us; first it washes us, and then it waters us, quenches our thirst, and supplies life to us. After passing through this experience for half an hour, we neither say that we are the best nor that we are the worst. Whether we are good or bad no longer matters; we are in another realm where there is the flow of living water. Even one who has not been saved very long has had this experience in the church. Perhaps some are not very clear and cannot put their experience into words, but in this chapter I am telling them their own story. This is not according to my imagination, because I have the same story that they do. I have been saved for fifty-two years. For many years I have been enlightened and burned, and I have enjoyed the flowing of life. This is not something we experience once for all. Rather, it is something from which we never graduate.

We cannot graduate from breathing, drinking, or eating. Once we graduate from these things, we are finished. Likewise, we cannot graduate from spiritual experiences. We may illustrate our experience in this way: In the morning, a young brother may have the shining, burning, and flowing for half an hour, and he feels wonderful and shouts Hallelujah! However, this Hallelujah lasts at most until noon. At lunch time, for some unexplainable reason, he becomes offended with someone at the table. Due to this, the water no longer flows within him, and there is no more shining or burning; everything is dark again. While others are shouting Hallelujah, he cannot say anything. Even if he tries to say Amen, it comes out unnaturally, and he feels sick. However, after another two days, he attends morning watch again—thank the Lord for the blessed morning watch, a place of blessing. In the first two minutes of the morning watch, while others are saying Hallelujah, Amen, he feels awkward, but morning watch is a place to be enlightened. Soon the light comes, and he begins to blame himself again. He feels that he should not have blamed this one or that one. It is not that the cook did not cook properly or that the one at lunch was wrong. Rather, he was offended because he was wrong, peculiar, unwilling to get into the flow, and reluctant to submit to others. He even feels that he is detestable. He beats his breast and abhors himself. After five minutes he is burning again, and after a few more minutes everything is burned away. Now there is a real Hallelujah within him. After this burning, everything within him is clear, refreshing, and wonderful. His thirst is quenched, and he is satisfied and watered.

This experience may last from morning to evening. In the evening, however, when the young brother comes into the meeting, an usher who is unaware that he is a newborn babe compels him to sit in the balcony away from the center. This causes the brother to suffer a "relapse" of his "ailment." He begins to murmur, "What kind of an usher is this? What kind of arrangement is this? Why do I have to be forced to sit in a certain place? I will complain to the elders!" Because of this, he cannot receive anything in the meeting, and after he goes home, he is so angry that he cannot sleep the whole night. He is even angry the next day, but thank the Lord, a person who is saved by grace eventually enjoys grace. After another period of being disturbed, he goes to morning watch again, even though he is still unhappy. While sitting there, he does not open his heart or his mouth, but after five minutes he is enlightened and says to himself, "Oh, I am so wicked! Why couldn't I be regulated by the usher? If everyone here were like me, there would be no way to have a meeting." After this enlightening, he is burned again. This time the burning is so fierce that he bursts out crying, "O Lord, no one is as wicked as I am. I do not deserve to be here!" Finally, after weeping, he begins to rejoice. He has the living water; he is watered, his thirst is quenched, and he has peace. This time his experience may last for over three days. In those three days he shouts Hallelujahs as if he has soared into heaven. He is so happy that he testifies wherever he goes, "The church life is really wonderful. You all have to come to the church!" After a few days, however, his wife observes that he is not doing anything except rejoicing, and she begins to rebuke him. At first he does not mind, but after more nagging, the "thorn bush" in him is ignited again, he becomes angry, and he says to his wife, "What is the matter with you? Are you not happy that I have been blessed so much? What are you complaining about?" Thus, he suffers another relapse.

Even if you allowed me, I could not finish this story; it goes on and on. Some may ask where I learned all these things. Actually, I am not talking about someone else; I am talking about myself. Again and again I have had this kind of experience. The best part, however, is that the enlightening, burning, and flowing lasts only a few hours the first time, but the second time it increases to half a day, and the third time it lasts over three days. Soon it will last for two weeks and then two months. It will last longer and longer until there is no time left for a "relapse." I am a frequent traveler, and I need to get an immunization against smallpox every time I travel. The earliest shot I had for smallpox was when I was a child, but when I was going to travel at the age of thirty or forty, I needed to be inoculated again. Since it had been thirty years since my first inoculation, I broke out with a great red swelling on my arm. After another period of time, when I received another shot, the size of the swelling was smaller. When I was inoculated recently before coming to Taipei, there was no swelling at all. After more than seventy years, there is no more outbreak. It is exactly the same in spiritual things. Today if you bother me, it is not so easy for me to lose my temper. In the past, every time after I lost my temper there was the shining of light; after the shining, there was the burning; and after the burning, there was the washing and watering. After many repeated experiences over the years, today there is no more "outbreak." This is the situation of some of the brothers and sisters among us who have been experiencing the Lord for many years. They can be "inoculated" without any swelling.

When their spouse rebukes them, their temper is not stirred up. They still say Hallelujah regardless of how others treat them.

IN THE NEW JERUSALEM
THERE BEING ONLY A RIVER OF WATER OF LIFE

The Spirit never fails to flow after He burns in us; His flowing always follows His burning. Whether there is more burning after the flowing depends on whether there is anything more in us that needs burning. The burning will go on until everything is burned away. If one day we do not become angry, regardless of how others treat us, then we need no further burning. At this stage there is only the flowing. When we reach this stage, we are the New Jerusalem. In the New Jerusalem the burning does not follow the watering. In the New Jerusalem there is only a river of water of life flowing for eternity. There will be no more burning, because the burning Spirit has become the flowing Spirit. There will be a river of water of life, bright as crystal, flowing to eternity.

None among us has reached such a stage, but thank the Lord, we are on the way. We are assured that we are on the way, but many who are in the denominations do not have the same assurance. Many of them do not have the enlightening, the burning, or the flowing. It is only when we enter into these subjective experiences that we have first the seven shining lamps, then the seven lamps of fire, and then the lamps of fire becoming a river. There is a river of water of life flowing in us for us to be watered, saturated, and supplied and for us to supply others. This is the reality in the church. Today the church in a proper condition is the New Jerusalem. Some of us are not yet in Revelation 21 and 22. Instead, some are still in Revelation 4 with lightnings, voices, thunders, and seven lamps of fire burning before the throne. However, we must not forget that Revelation 4 is heading toward Revelation 21 and 22. Chapter 4 is not the end but the process; the end is in chapters 21 and 22. In Revelation 21 and 22 the throne in chapter 4 reappears. It is still the same throne, but what proceeds from it is not fire but a flow.

Today in the church we should have this kind of testimony

and this kind of living. Among us we should have not only the lamps shining and the fire burning but also the living water flowing. When fire is needed, there is fire, and when water is needed, there is water, but fire is not the goal; it is the procedure. Water is the goal. The ultimate goal of the church is that people are brought into the flow of the living water. "The Spirit and the bride say, Come! And let him who hears say, Come! And let him who is thirsty come; let him who wills take the water of life freely" (22:17). This is salvation, this is the gospel, and this is the church life.

At the beginning of Revelation, the Lamb has seven eyes, which are the seven Spirits, and the seven Spirits are the burning lamps, but at the end of Revelation, the lamp is the Lamb. When we reach this stage, we are in eternity. In the New Jerusalem there is only the need for the lamp; there is no further need for fire. In the New Jerusalem there is light but not fire, and the New Jerusalem is full of water. At present, the church has the shining and the burning, but the burning becomes the flowing of water. God is the light, Christ is the lamp, and the Spirit is the flowing water. This is the Triune God. When the church is mature and enters into a proper condition, there will be only light and water. There will be no fire, because there will be no more defeated ones, degraded ones, or backsliding ones. We will only need the light to shine for our move and the water to supply us; we will not need fire to judge or burn us. This is the condition of the New Jerusalem. Thank the Lord, today in the church we can have a foretaste of the New Jerusalem. In such a church there is light and water but no fire, because all the fire is in the lake of fire. Everything has been judged; all that is left is God's presence. In the presence of God, He is the light and Christ is the lamp, and out from Him flows the Spirit as our living water. This is our experience in the church.

ABOUT THE AUTHOR

Witness Lee was born in 1905 in northern China and raised in a Christian family. At age 19 he was fully captured for Christ and immediately consecrated himself to preach the gospel for the rest of his life. Early in his service, he met Watchman Nee, a renowned preacher, teacher, and writer. Witness Lee labored together with Watchman Nee under his direction. In 1934 Watchman Nee entrusted Witness Lee with the responsibility for his publication operation, called the Shanghai Gospel Bookroom.

Prior to the Communist takeover in 1949, Witness Lee was sent by Watchman Nee and his other co-workers to Taiwan to ensure that the things delivered to them by the Lord would not be lost. Watchman Nee instructed Witness Lee to continue the former's publishing operation abroad as the Taiwan Gospel Bookroom, which has been publicly recognized as the publisher of Watchman Nee's works outside China. Witness Lee's work in Taiwan manifested the Lord's abundant blessing. From a mere 350 believers, newly fled from the mainland, the churches in Taiwan grew to 20,000 in five years.

In 1962 Witness Lee felt led of the Lord to come to the United States, and he began to minister in Los Angeles. During his 35 years of service in the U.S., he ministered in weekly meetings and weekend conferences, delivering several thousand spoken messages. Much of his speaking has since been published as over 400 titles. Many of these have been translated into over fourteen languages. He gave his last public conference in February 1997 at the age of 91.

He leaves behind a prolific presentation of the truth in the Bible. His major work, *Life-study of the Bible,* comprises over 25,000 pages of commentary on every book of the Bible from the perspective of the believers' enjoyment and experience of God's divine life in Christ through the Holy Spirit. Witness Lee was the chief editor of a new translation of the New Testament into Chinese called the Recovery Version and directed the translation of the same into English. The Recovery Version also appears in a number of other languages. He provided an extensive body of footnotes, outlines, and spiritual cross references. A radio broadcast of his messages can be heard on Christian radio stations in the United States. In 1965 Witness Lee founded Living Stream Ministry, a non-profit corporation, located in Anaheim, California, which officially presents his and Watchman Nee's ministry.

Witness Lee's ministry emphasizes the experience of Christ as life and the practical oneness of the believers as the Body of Christ. Stressing the importance of attending to both these matters, he led the churches under his care to grow in Christian life and function. He was unbending in his conviction that God's goal is not narrow sectarianism but the Body of Christ. In time, believers began to meet simply as the church in their localities in response to this conviction. In recent years a number of new churches have been raised up in Russia and in many European countries.

OTHER BOOKS PUBLISHED BY
Living Stream Ministry

Titles by Witness Lee:

Abraham—Called by God	978-0-7363-0359-0
The Experience of Life	978-0-87083-417-2
The Knowledge of Life	978-0-87083-419-6
The Tree of Life	978-0-87083-300-7
The Economy of God	978-0-87083-415-8
The Divine Economy	978-0-87083-268-0
God's New Testament Economy	978-0-87083-199-7
The World Situation and God's Move	978-0-87083-092-1
Christ vs. Religion	978-0-87083-010-5
The All-inclusive Christ	978-0-87083-020-4
Gospel Outlines	978-0-87083-039-6
Character	978-0-87083-322-9
The Secret of Experiencing Christ	978-0-87083-227-7
The Life and Way for the Practice of the Church Life	978-0-87083-785-2
The Basic Revelation in the Holy Scriptures	978-0-87083-105-8
The Crucial Revelation of Life in the Scriptures	978-0-87083-372-4
The Spirit with Our Spirit	978-0-87083-798-2
Christ as the Reality	978-0-87083-047-1
The Central Line of the Divine Revelation	978-0-87083-960-3
The Full Knowledge of the Word of God	978-0-87083-289-5
Watchman Nee—A Seer of the Divine Revelation ...	978-0-87083-625-1

Titles by Watchman Nee:

How to Study the Bible	978-0-7363-0407-8
God's Overcomers	978-0-7363-0433-7
The New Covenant	978-0-7363-0088-9
The Spiritual Man • 3 volumes	978-0-7363-0269-2
Authority and Submission	978-0-7363-0185-5
The Overcoming Life	978-1-57593-817-2
The Glorious Church	978-0-87083-745-6
The Prayer Ministry of the Church	978-0-87083-860-6
The Breaking of the Outer Man and the Release ...	978-1-57593-955-1
The Mystery of Christ	978-1-57593-954-4
The God of Abraham, Isaac, and Jacob	978-0-87083-932-0
The Song of Songs	978-0-87083-872-9
The Gospel of God • 2 volumes	978-1-57593-953-7
The Normal Christian Church Life	978-0-87083-027-3
The Character of the Lord's Worker	978-1-57593-322-1
The Normal Christian Faith	978-0-87083-748-7
Watchman Nee's Testimony	978-0-87083-051-8

Available at
Christian bookstores, or contact Living Stream Ministry
2431 W. La Palma Ave. • Anaheim, CA 92801
1-800-549-5164 • www.livingstream.com